CONTENTS

DEDICATION	iii
ACKNOWLEDGMENTS	iv
INTRODUCTION	1

1. GLOSSARY OF TERMS — 3
- Netting — 3
- Selvedge — 3
- Direction of braid — 3
- Direction of netting — 3
- Panel — 3
- Sewing — 3
- Braiding — 3
- Row — 3
- Needle — 3
- Bar — 3
- Points — 3
- Clean meshes — 4
- Mesh size — 4
- Lead line: — 5
- Handline — 5
- Pockets — 5
- Mounting — 5
- Hanging — 5

2. NECESSARY EQUIPMENT AND MATERIALS — 6
- Equipment — 6
  - *Meshing needle* — 6
  - *Waistline* — 6
  - *Threading tool* — 7
  - *Wall hook* — 7
  - *Scissor* — 7
  - *Mosquito coil* — 7
  - *Mesh stick* — 7
- Material — 8
  - *Twine* — 8
  - *Rope* — 8
  - *Cord* — 8
  - *Netting* — 9
  - *Swivel* — 9
  - *Lead weights* — 9

3. COUNTING MESHES — 10

4. CAST NET PATTERNS — 11
- Multifilament cast net patterns — 12
- Monofilament cast net patterns — 13

5. CUTTING — 14
- All-cleaned mesh cutting — 14
- All-points mesh cutting — 16
- All-bars mesh cutting — 17

6. SEWING — 18
- Knots used in the sewing (braiding) process — 18
- Starting and finishing knot — 18
- Knot used to pick up two meshes — 19
- Side knot — 19
- Flat knot — 20
- Clove hitch with a half-hitch lock — 20
- Slipped half knot — 21
- Sheet bend — 21
- Fundamental knot-tying techniques — 22
- Sewing an all-points mesh cut — 25
- Sewing an all-cleaned mesh cut — 27

7. SWIVEL AND HANDLINE ATTACHMENT	**30**
Attaching the swivel to the net	30
Attaching the handline to the swivel	33
Rope terminology	33
Lay	33
Working end	33
Standing part	33
Splicing an eye in a rope	33
8. HANGING THE LEAD LINE	**37**
9. FORMING POCKETS	**42**
10. CASTING TECHNIQUES	**46**
Technique one	47
Technique two	51

11. MENDING CAST NETS	**55**
Trimming the tear	56
Horizontal tear	57
Vertical tear	58
Oblique tear	59
Repairing large tears	64
Tips for repairing small tears	66
Combination repair	66
12. MAKING A CAST NET TO SUIT YOUR INDIVIDUAL NEEDS	**68**
13. HOW A NET WORKS	**70**
14. CARE AND MAINTENANCE	**71**
CONCLUSION	**72**
REFERENCES	**73**

DEDICATION

I would like to dedicate this book to my grandfather, Ronald James McFarlane (1928–2020), who fostered my love for fishing by teaching me all his fishing secrets, as well as everything I know about making cast nets.

And to my grandmother, Charlotte Evelyn McFarlane (formally Drury; 1928–present), who was always able to put together something for us to eat on many a fishing trip, whether it be a big family trip at the beach or just a few of us in the boat, it was always enough to get us through the day. Grandma also liked wetting a line, and I often recall her pulling in a fish or two with Granddad's old timber reel handlines.

I will never forget the day that Granddad gave me my first cast net; I was about 11 or 12 years old. Those early days rubbed off on me, as I still extensively use a cast net to gather bait, as well as timber reel handlines to catch fish.

Up until recently, my grandfather still made cast nets and casts them, being the principle bait catcher whenever we had a chance to go fishing together.

To both of you, I thank you for your time and patience.

ACKNOWLEDGMENTS

I would like to thank my wife for helping me take the photos for this book, and for supporting me in writing this book. I would also like to thank my friends and family who have supported me along the way.

INTRODUCTION

A cast net, also known as a throw net, is generally used for fishing. It is a circular net with small weights distributed evenly around the outer perimeter of the net.

The net is cast or thrown by hand in such a manner that it spreads out on the water and sinks. Fish are trapped in the net and hauled back in. This simple device is particularly effective for catching small bait and pan-size fish, and has been in use, with various modifications, for thousands of years.

Cast nets were originally made from linen, which was then replaced by cotton until about the 1940 and 1950s, where a man-made synthetic fiber called nylon replaced it to this day. While multifilament nylon is still available, there is a strong preference for monofilament nylon cast nets, particularly in Australia.

With the advent of this man-made fiber, not only did it add to the strength of the net, it was also practically impervious to rot, reducing the care and treatment required to gain longevity of the net.

To this day, I have a multifilament nylon cast net that is more than 25 years old. I still use this net, but I have repaired it many times.

MY CAST NET HISTORY

My grandfather has been making cast nets since he was about 12 years old (over 75 years). He was taught by his father (Arthur McFarlane), but not by the method shown in this book. You see, back then the availability of machine-made net was nonexistent, so fishermen would literally have to make a cast net from a ball of string.

This particular process is started by braiding a small number of meshes, of a chosen mesh size, into a circle, and then working around the circumference of this circle, braiding on additional meshes, and thus growing the cast net into the desired diameter/spread. I must admit that I have never made a cast net using this method; however, I am fully aware of the process.

My history with making cast nets only dates back to 1989, when I was 20 years old. Between my great-grandfather, grandfather and myself, the three of us have well over 100 years of experience and would have made hundreds of cast nets.

While I have stopped making cast nets for other people, my grandfather still made them up until his recent passing. He has made them for people as far away as Western Australia and the Northern Territory, but predominately they are Queensland-based fishermen who are based around the Ingham district that he resided in. His nests are well-sought after due to their superior quality and strength over the more commercially available cast nets.

FISHING REGULATIONS

Regulations differ between countries, states and territories. So it would be prudent of you to investigate the fishing laws that are applicable to where you live.

Some states in Australia do not allow the use of a cast net, while others allow their use, but at restricted mesh and net sizes. In Queensland, Australia, the maximum mesh size is 28 mm (1 & ⅛ of an inch) and the maximum length is 3.7 m (~12 foot) when measured from the point of attachment of the cord or rope to the net lead line or bottom of the lowest pocket of the net, whichever is greater.

Refer to diagrams on the right.

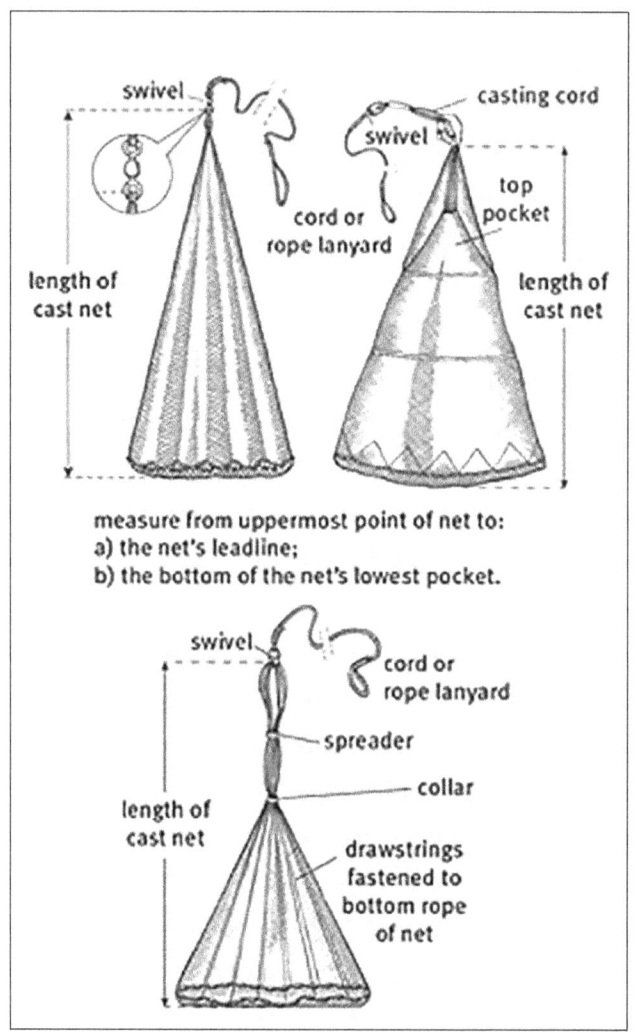

Measuring dimensions of cast nets (Queensland, Australia). Reference: Queensland Government – Department of Agriculture, Fisheries and Forestry.

2   MAKING AND MENDING CAST NETS

1. GLOSSARY OF TERMS

NETTING: This is the material out of which a cast net is constructed. It can be purchased in various lengths, depths and mesh sizes.

SELVEDGE: Refers to the outer perimeter of a net. It can be either 'single selvedge' or 'double selvedge', as shown in **Figure 1**. Double selvedge is generally used where the outer edge of the net is subject to more wear and tear.

DIRECTION OF BRAID: This refers to the direction that the netting was braided in – left to right or right to left – and is parallel to the rows of the netting. Refer to **Figure 1**.

DIRECTION OF NETTING: This refers to the increase in the depth of the netting as each row is braided on, and is perpendicular to the rows of the netting. Refer to **Figure 1**.

PANEL: A panel is a rectangular section of netting; its dimensions are expressed in the number of meshes counted in the direction of the braid and the direction of the netting.

SEWING: This is the process used to join panels.

BRAIDING: This is the process used to create rows and meshes.

ROW: A row is a series of half meshes aligned in the direction of the braid. Two successive rows have to be braided together to increase the depth of a panel by one mesh.

NEEDLE: The implement used to hold a suitable amount of twine for the sewing and braiding process.

BAR: These are the tags that are produced when a net is cut obliquely to the direction of braid and the direction of the netting. Refer to **Figure 1**.

POINTS: These are the tags that are produced when a net is cut in the direction of the netting. Refer to **Figure 1**.

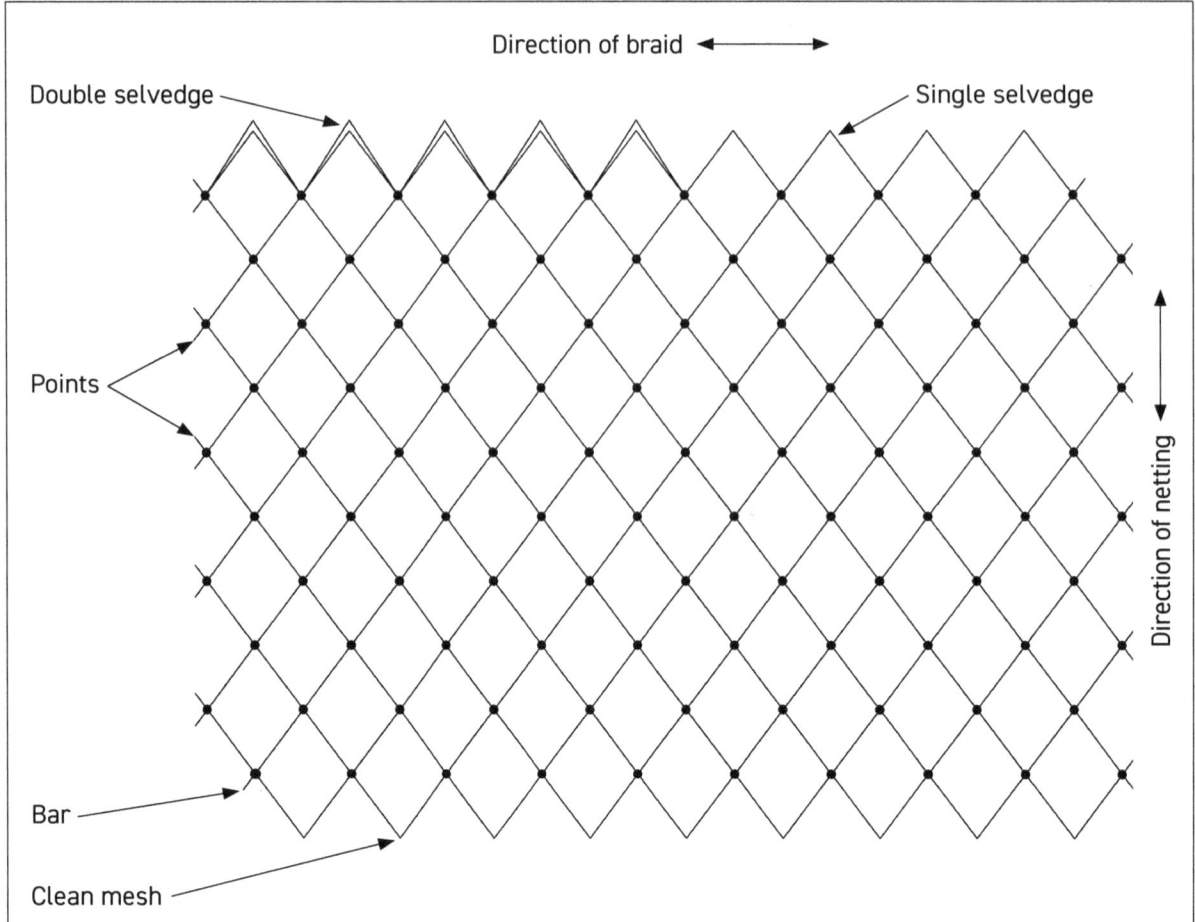

Figure 1

CLEAN MESHES: These are produced when the net is cut in such a way as to produce a mesh with no knot. Refer to **Figure 1**. This cutting process will be discussed in depth in Chapter 5. Note that a clean mesh can only be produced when the meshes are cut in the direction of the braid.

MESH SIZE: There are various methods used for measuring mesh size by different authorities. For the sake of simplicity, only the 'stretched-mesh' method will be referred to throughout this book, as it generally aligns to most manufacturers and authorities. The mesh opening is measured in the stretched-mesh method and is the length between two opposing knots when the mesh is stretched, as shown in **Figure 1.1**.

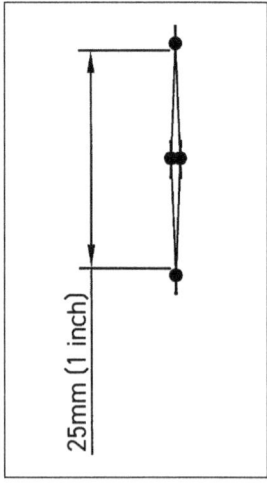

Figure 1.1

LEAD LINE: The lead line is attached to the outer circumference of the cast net. It is made up of a small diameter cord and lead weights that are distributed evenly around the outer perimeter of the cast net. Refer to **Figure 1.2**.

HANDLINE: This is the rope that connects you – the user – to the cast net itself. Refer to **Figure 1.2**.

POCKETS: These are produced by hemming the outer edge of the cast net at individual points, so as to produce a pocket on the inside of the cast net. Pockets aid in the capture of fish. Refer to **Figure 1.3**.

MOUNTING: The attachment of netting to a support rope.

HANGING: The mounting of the netting according to a specific relationship between the length of the support rope and the length of the netting.

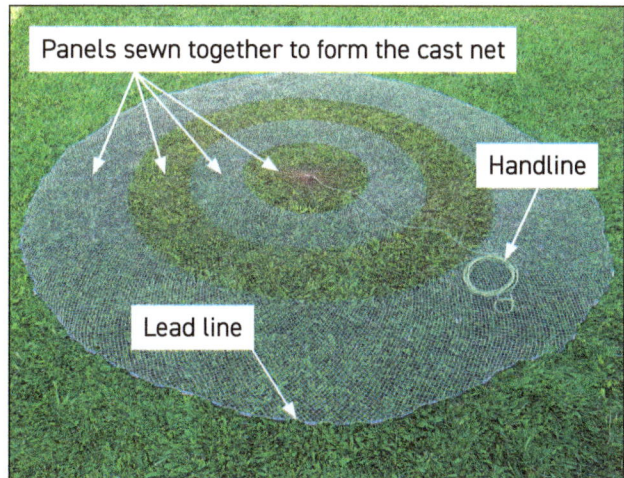

Figure 1.2

Figure 1.3

2. NECESSARY EQUIPMENT AND MATERIALS

EQUIPMENT

MESHING NEEDLE

Meshing needles can come in many forms. I will depict two in this section.

One is commercially available in most tackle stores, see **Figure 2**, and the other one I fabricate myself and personally prefer to use, as it is far more suitable for small meshes, which cast nets are principally made from. An aluminium knitting needle can be formed into the home-made meshing needle shown in **Figure 2.1**.

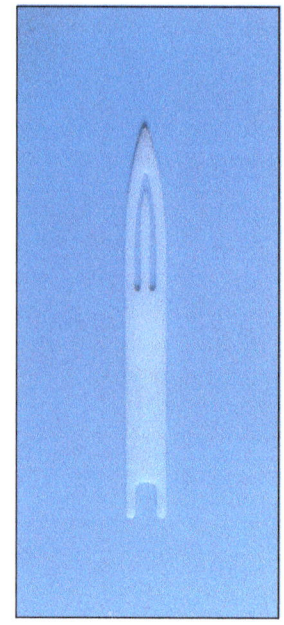

Figure 2   Figure 2.1

At least two meshing needles are required. One smaller needle 150–200 mm (6–8 inches) long, made from a 3–4 mm (⅛ to ⁵⁄₃₂ of an inch) diameter rod for sewing the panels of netting together. And one larger needle 200–250 mm (8–10 inches) long, made from a 5–6 mm (⁷⁄₃₂–¼ of an inch) diameter rod for hanging the lead line and pockets of the cast net.

WAISTLINE

This is a piece of cord used to aid in the sewing and braiding process. As the name implies, it is tied around your waist, while at the same time holding a section of netting. You will need to cut the waistline to a length that is comfortable for your own use. Refer to **Figure 2.2**.

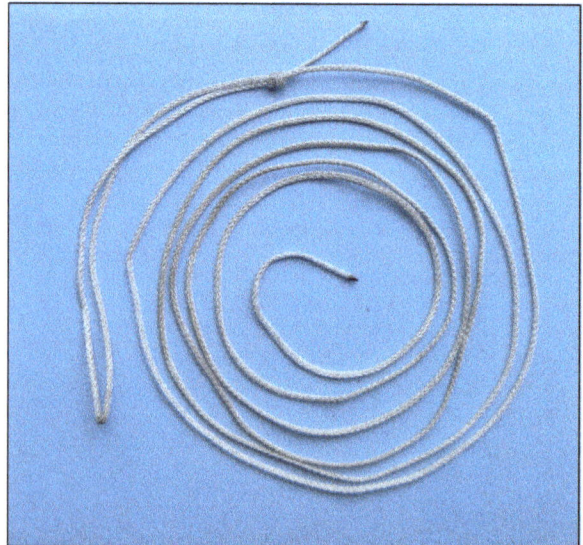

Figure 2.2

THREADING TOOL

This is used to thread the waistline through the meshes of a pre-cut panel of net.

It is approximately 300 mm (1 foot) long, and 6 mm (1/4 of an inch) in diameter. An aluminium knitting needle can be formed into the threading tool shown in **Figure 2.3**.

Figure 2.3

WALL HOOK

These are used to assist in the sewing process and for hanging the lead line. A hook diameter of approximately 20 mm should suffice. Refer to **Figure 2.4**.

Figure 2.4

SCISSOR

It is essential that these are of good quality and sharp, as it makes the task of cutting the net into panels a lot easier. Refer to **Figure 2.5**.

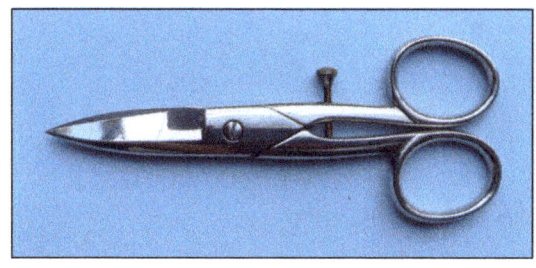

Figure 2.5

MOSQUITO COIL

I suppose this seems like an unusual item, but its purpose is to seal the ends of the nylon netting once it has been cut, in order to prevent fraying. Refer to **Figure 2.6**. Oh yeah, and it keeps the mosquitoes away too!

MESH STICK

This is used to aid in the hand braiding of rows and meshes. It is generally made from a piece of wood 100 mm (4 inches) long with a cross section, which varies to suit the size of the mesh being made. The perimeter of the cross section is equal to the size of the mesh. Mesh sticks are numbered according to the size of the mesh they make, thus a No. 2.5 mesh stick will produce a 2.5-cm or 25-mm mesh size. **Figure 2.7** shows a homemade mesh stick that will produce a 25-mm (1 inch) mesh.

Figure 2.6

Figure 2.7

MAKING AND MENDING CAST NETS

MATERIAL

Most of the below materials can be purchased through your local hardware and tackle stores.

TWINE

Used for sewing the panels of net together. Use 210/6-ply nylon twine for multifilament nylon cast nets or 5-kg monofilament fishing line for monofilament cast nets. For hanging the lead line and forming the pockets, use 210/18-ply nylon twine or 12-ply polyethylene twine. **Figure 2.8** shows a roll of multifilament nylon twine. **Figure 2.9** shows a roll of monofilament fishing line and **Figure 2.10** shows a roll of polyethylene twine.

ROPE

This is for the handline. Use 4-mm polypropylene rope that is 6 m long. Refer to **Figure 2.11**.

CORD

This is for the lead line. Use 2-mm or 2.5-mm diameter nylon braided venetian blind cord, or 30-ply polyethylene cord to be used for the lead line. **Figure 2.12** shows a roll of venetian blind cord and **Figure 2.13** shows a roll of 30-ply polyethylene cord.

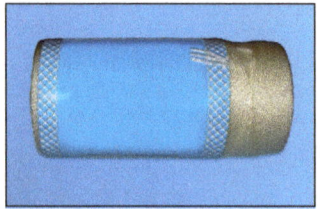
Figure 2.8

Figure 2.9

Figure 2.10

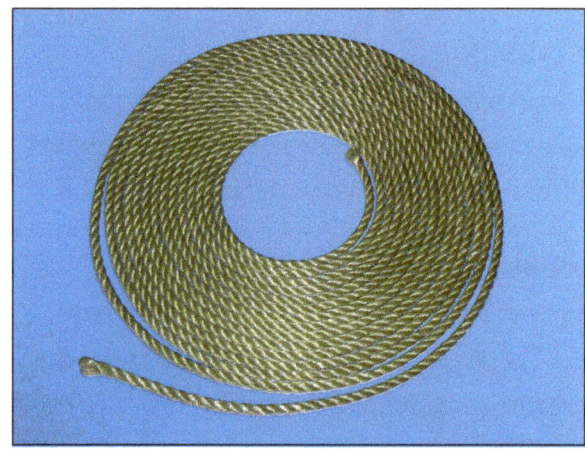
Figure 2.11

Figure 2.12

Figure 2.13

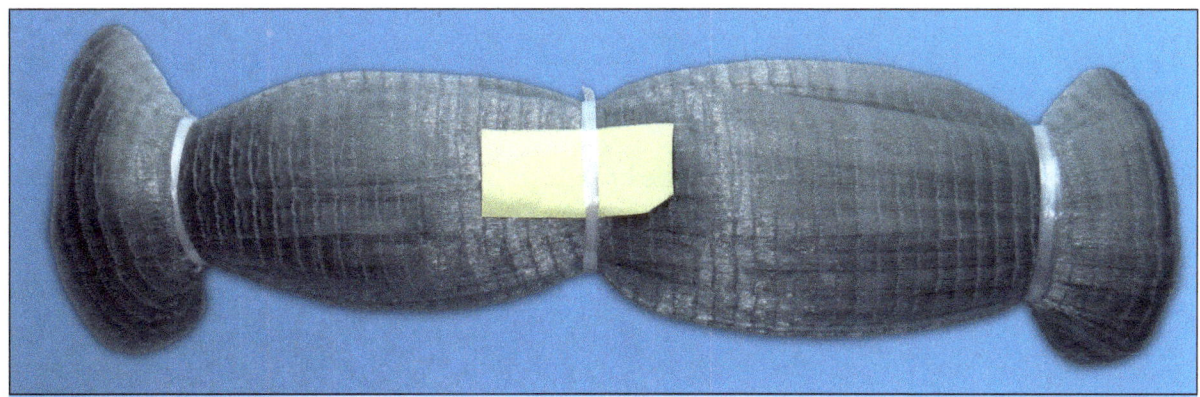

Figure 2.14

NETTING

One bundle of 210/6-ply nylon net with a 25-mm (1 inch) mesh size, 100 meshes deep and 50 m (54 yards) long, or No4 line monofilament with the same mesh size, depth and length. As this book focuses on cast nets for 'general use', a bundle with a 25-mm mesh size is recommended. As a guide, a bundle of net of this size will be enough to construct approximately four 12-foot spread cast nets. Alternatively, an old disused drag net may be used for your first foray into the world of making cast nets. Refer to **Figure 2.14**.

Figure 2.15

SWIVEL

Use a No8 or No9 torpedo swivel for joining the handline to the top of the cast net. Refer to **Figure 2.15**.

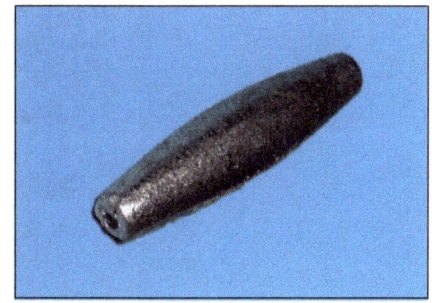

Figure 2.16

LEAD WEIGHTS

No4 barrel sinkers with a modified 3-mm hole, or homemade lead weights 38 mm long with a 3-mm hole and 8-mm diameter. **Figure 2.16** shows a No4 barrel sinker, and **Figure 2.17** shows a homemade lead weight that I made.

Figure 2.17

3. COUNTING MESHES

Before any cutting can be performed on the bundle of net, it is necessary to understand how to count the meshes.

We will start by defining a 'whole mesh' and a 'half mesh', as shown in **Figure 3**.

A whole mesh is defined as having four sides that join together to form a diamond shape.

Whereas a half mesh is generally defined as having two sides that join together to form only half of the diamond shape.

As you can see in **Figure 3**, we have nine and a half meshes in the direction of the braid, and five and a half meshes in the direction of the netting.

The reasoning behind the half mesh will become more apparent in Chapter 6, the sewing process. Here we actually sew in the other half of the mesh to form a whole mesh.

Note that the half mesh may be counted, either at the start or at the end.

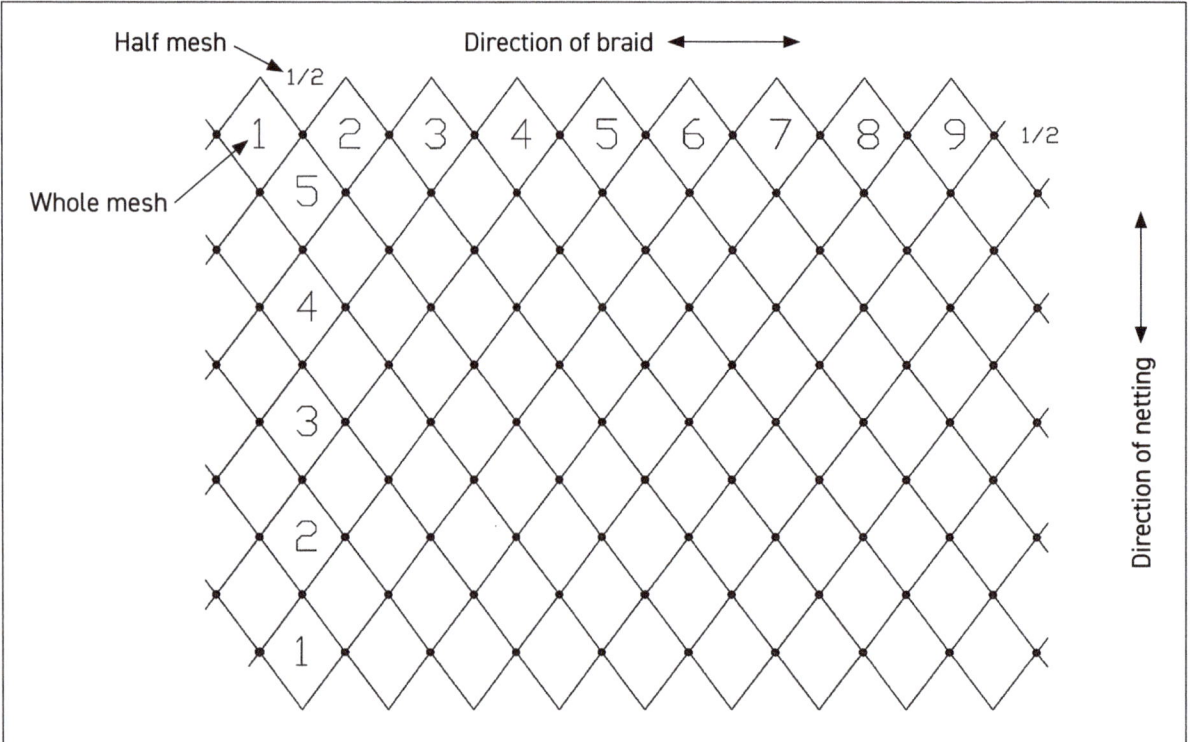

Figure 3

10   MAKING AND MENDING CAST NETS

4. CAST NET PATTERNS

These cutting patterns have been refined over many years by trial and error. The primary goal is to develop a cast net that uses the least amount of material, while at the same time producing a quality net that spreads easily. The depths also fit well for reducing the amount of net wastage by having the depth divide evenly into a standard bundle of net, at 100-meshes deep.

The first net patterns **(Table 4.1)** are for multifiliment nylon cast nets, while the second net patterns **(Table 4.2)** are for monofilament cast nets.

All net paterns below are based on a 25-mm (1 inch) mesh size.

Note that in the cast net world, we still have a tendency to use the old imperial system of feet and inches when refering to the spread diameter of a cast net – see tables below.

The following are some notes for reading the tables below.

DEPTH (direction of netting) and **LENGTH** (direction of braid) represent the number of meshes the panels are cut into (for more details, refer to Chapter 5, on cutting).

RATIO indicates when one mesh is required to be sewn to two meshes when joining panels.

So when you see a 1 in the table below, that means for every mesh you pick up on that corresponding panel, you will pick up two meshes on the panel below.

And when you see a 2 in the table below, that means for every second mesh you pick up on that corresponding panel, you will pick up two meshes on the panel below, and so on.

Figure 4 shows a graghical representation of ratios between panels.

NUMBER OF LEADS indicates the minimum number of leads required for each pattern.

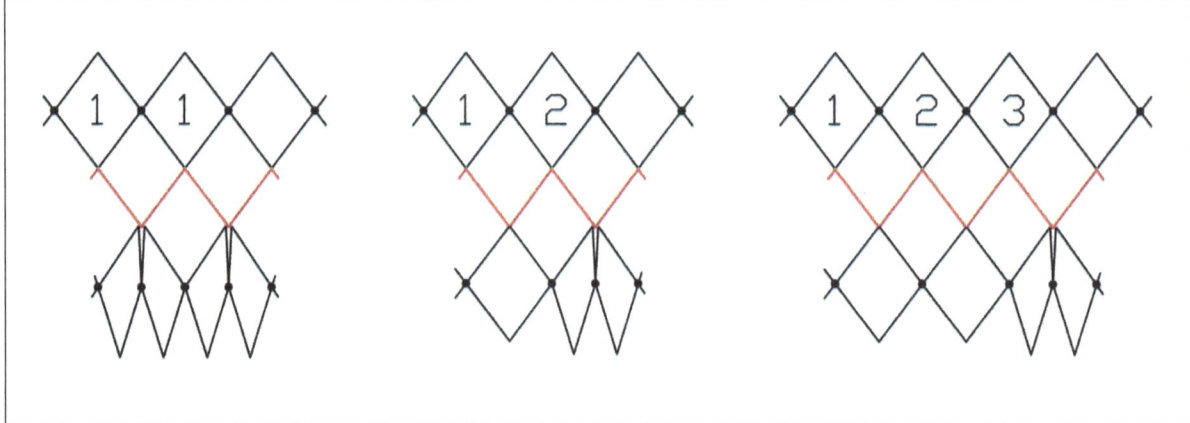

Figure 4

TABLE 4.1 MULTIFILAMENT CAST NET PATTERNS

10-foot spread (3.05 metres)			
Depth	Length	Ratio	Number of leads
12.5	95.5	1	
12.5	191.5	1	
24.5	383.5	2	
36.5	575.5		96

12-foot spread (3.66 metres)			
Depth	Length	Ratio	Number of leads
12.5	95.5	1	
12.5	191.5	2	
12.5	287.5	2	
24.5	431.5	2	
36.5	647.5		108

14-foot spread (4.27 metres)			
Depth	Length	Ratio	Number of leads
12.5	95.5	1	
12.5	191.5	2	
12.5	287.5	2	
12.5	431.5	3	
24.5	575.5	3	
36.5	767.5		128

16-foot spread (4.88 metres)			
Depth	Length	Ratio	Number of leads
12.5	95.5	1	
12.5	191.5	2	
12.5	287.5	3	
12.5	383.5	3	
12.5	511.5	3	
24.5	681.5	4	
36.5	851.5		142

TABLE 4.2 MONOFILAMENT CAST NET PATTERNS

10-foot spread (3.05 metres)			
Depth	Length	Ratio	Number of leads
5.5	159.5	1	
6.5	319.5	2	
12.5	479.5	3	
12.5	639.5	4	
12.5	799.5	5	
24.5	959.5		96

12-foot spread (3.66 metres)			
Depth	Length	Ratio	Number of leads
5.5	159.5	1	
6.5	319.5	2	
12.5	479.5	3	
12.5	639.5	4	
12.5	799.5	5	
12.5	959.5	6	
24.5	1119.5		112

14-foot spread (4.27 metres)			
Depth	Length	Ratio	Number of leads
5.5	159.5	1	
6.5	319.5	2	
12.5	479.5	3	
12.5	639.5	4	
12.5	799.5	5	
12.5	959.5	6	
12.5	1119.5	7	
24.5	1279.5		128

16-foot spread (4.88 metres)			
Depth	Length	Ratio	Number of leads
5.5	159.5	1	
6.5	319.5	2	
12.5	479.5	3	
12.5	639.5	4	
12.5	799.5	5	
12.5	959.5	6	
12.5	1119.5	7	
12.5	1279.5	8	
24.5	1439.5		144

You will have seen that a lot more net is required in the monofilament cast net patterns, compared to the multifilament cast net patterns. The reason for this is that the monofilament material resists spreading due to its spring-like nature. This is called the 'spring factor'. Most commercially available cast nets use No3 monofilament line, the reason being is that this lighter monofilament line will have a lower spring factor, allowing the net to spread out to its full potential more easily, while at the same time allowing the manufacturer to use less material.

Since the cast net patterns in this book are based on No4 monofilament line, they ultimately require more net in the design to create a cast net that will spread to its full potential.

I have chosen No4 monofilament line due to its additional strength (20% stronger), and ultimately its resistance to tearing.

5. CUTTING

At this point there are two terms you will need to know when cutting a net. They are 'direction of braid' and 'direction of netting'. Refer to Chapter 1, page 3.

The purpose of cutting a net is to produce rectangular panels of various sizes for constructing the cast net from. The rectangular panels are obtained by creating two 'all-cleaned mesh' cuts made in the direction of the braid, two 'all-points' cuts made in the direction of the netting, and two 'oblique' cuts producing a 'bar' in diagonally opposite corners of the panel. Refer to **Figure 5**.

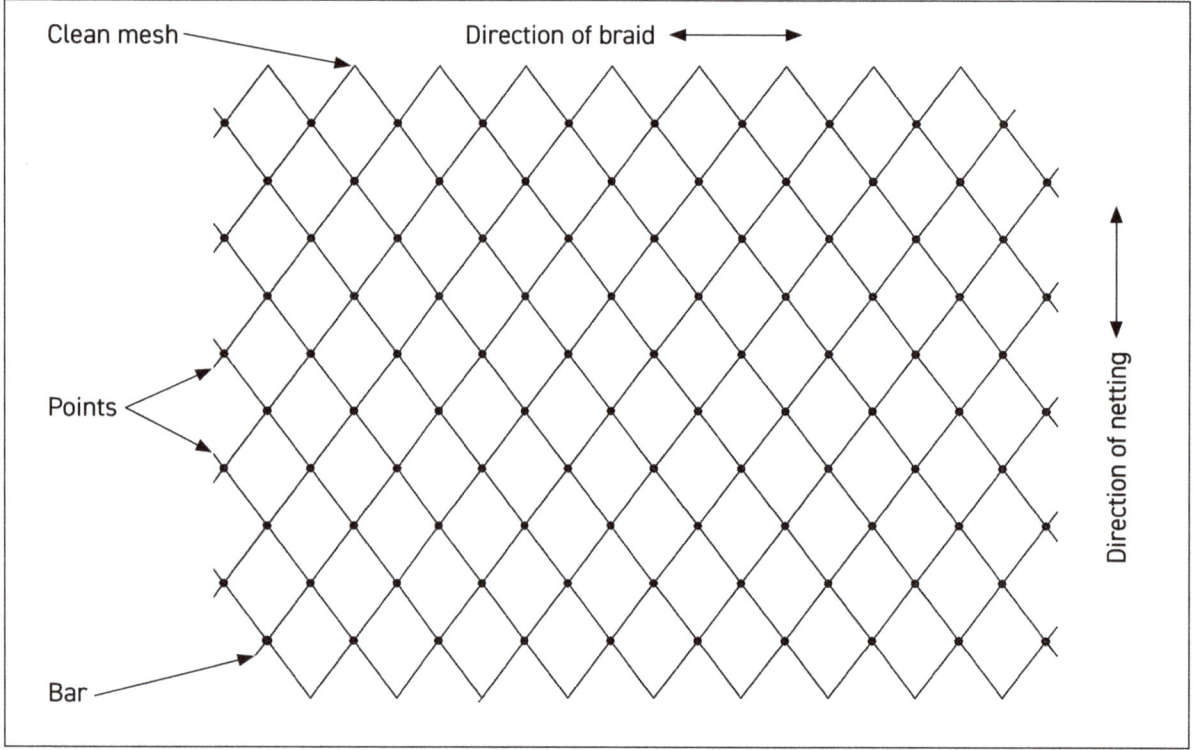

Figure 5

ALL-CLEANED MESH CUTTING

This cut is made in the direction of the braid, which is along the length of the net. To obtain a clean mesh when cutting out, it is necessary to cut as close to the base of the knot as possible, so as when the mesh is stretched the knot will undo, thus leaving a clean mesh. **Figure 5.1** shows the position of the cuts in order to produce an all-cleaned mesh cut. **Figure 5.2** shows the resultant rectangular panel with tags still to be removed.

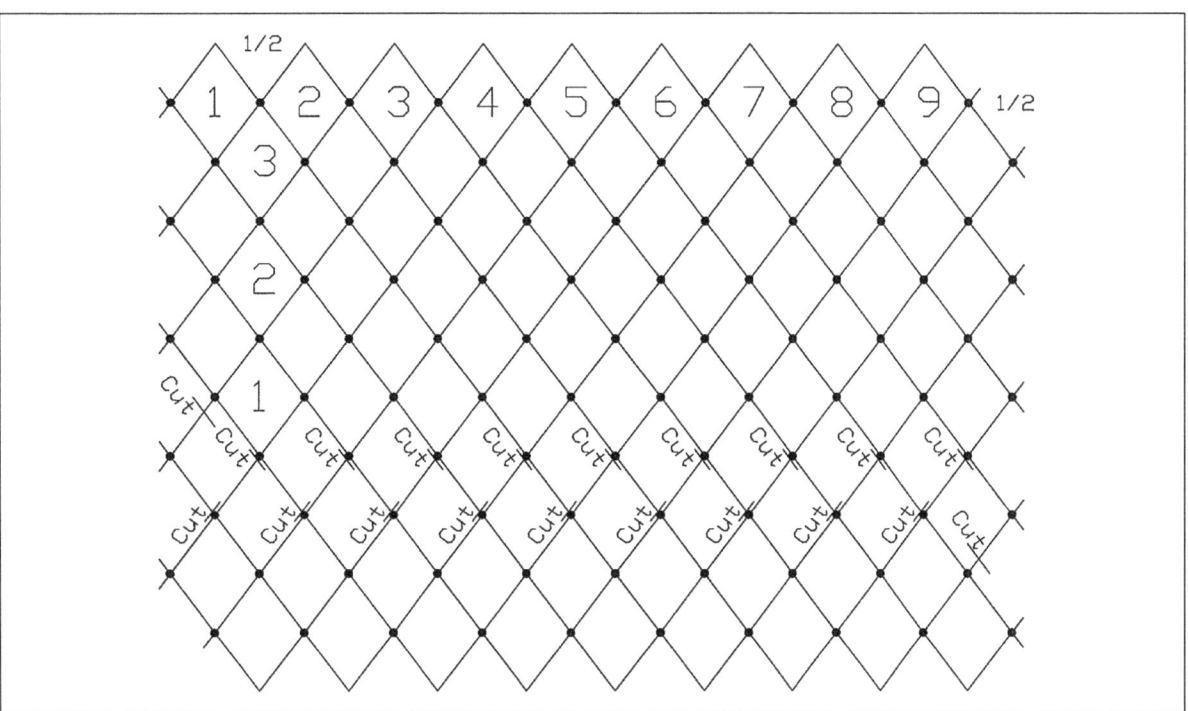

Figure 5.1

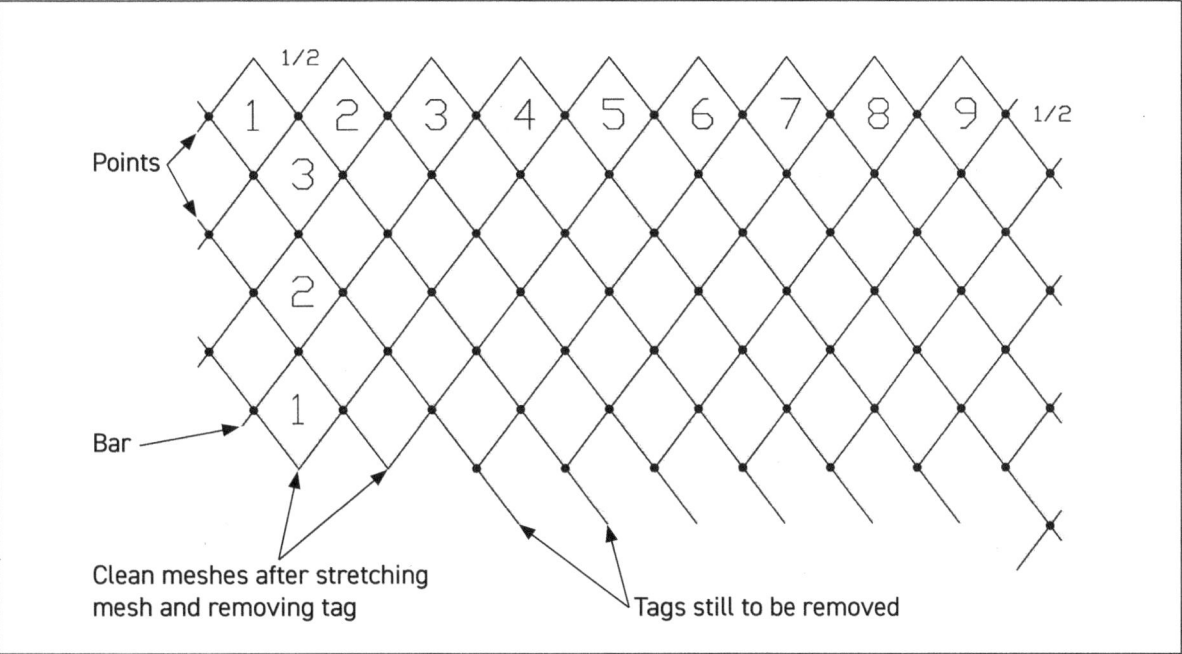

Figure 5.2

NOTE that sometimes the meshes may be difficult to clean. I've found that by turning the net over and cutting from the opposite side, the problem will generally be alleviated. If you are still having difficulty, check that the cut is made flush with the knot. There should be no tag protruding from the knot.

ALL-POINTS MESH CUTTING

This cut is made in the direction of the netting, along the depth of the net.

To obtain the all-points cut, it is necessary to place the cut through the centre of the mesh between diagonally opposite corners, as shown in **Figure 5.3**. With this cutting technique, it is not necessary to cut close to the base of the knot. In fact, it is important to leave two tab ends (known as 'points') to prevent the knot coming undone. **Figure 5.4** shows the finished product after the netting is cut away.

NOTE that if constructing a cast net from a multifilament nylon material, it is necessary to fuse the ends of the points to prevent fraying. Using a lit mosquito coil is perfect for this job; just wipe the hot end of the mosquito coil over the end of the point to fuse it sufficiently.

Figure 5.3

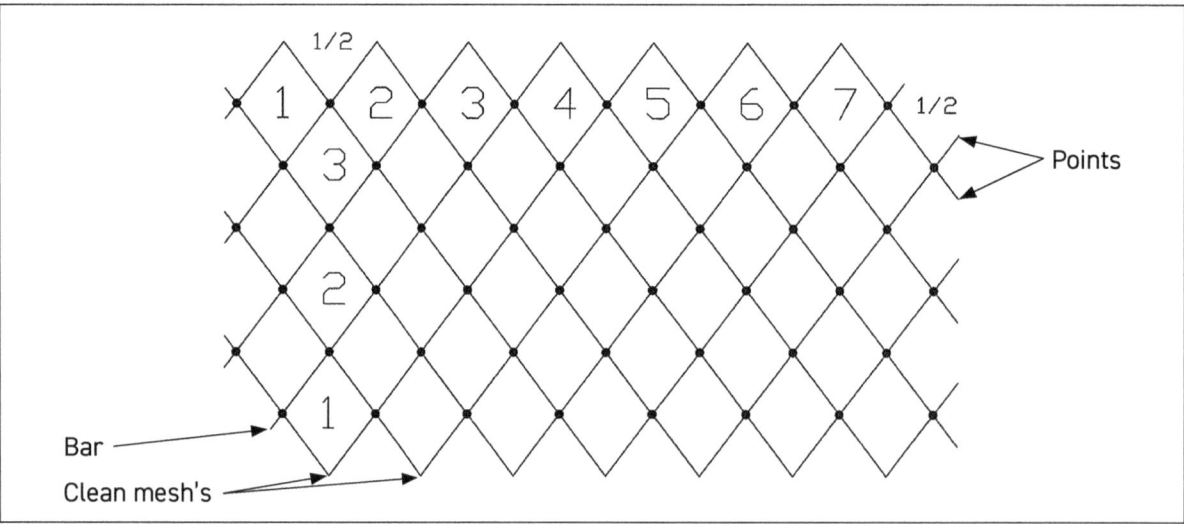

Figure 5.4

ALL-BARS MESH CUTTING

This cutting technique will have limited use with this particular type of cast net construction, but the knowledge is necessary nonetheless. To carry out this cutting technique, the cut is made obliquely across the net, as shown in **Figure 5.5**. This cut will produce the tag ends, which are called 'bars'.

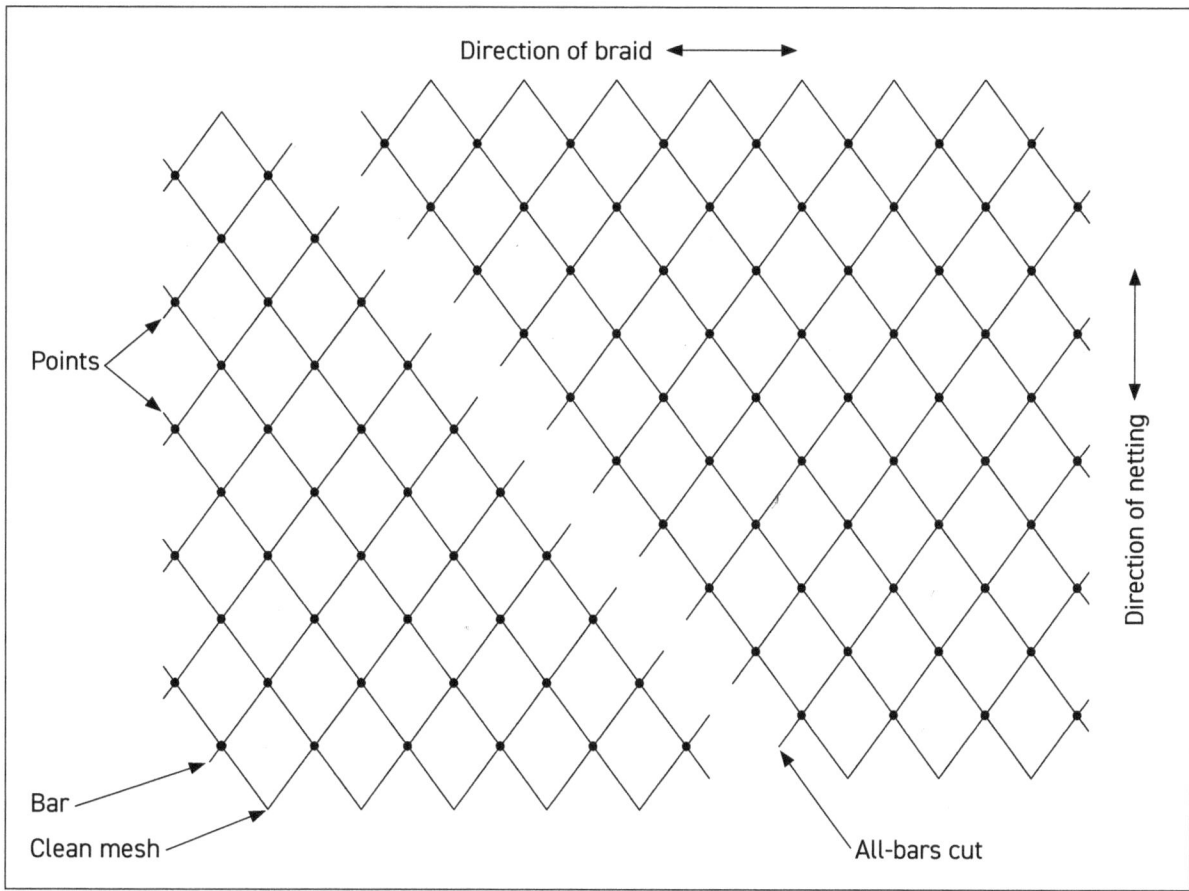

Figure 5.5

MAKING AND MENDING CAST NETS

6. SEWING

Now that you have cut the panels out for your net, it's time to sew them together.

But before we move on, I will show you a number of knots that you will need in order to sew the panels together. Note that when reading the diagrams below and you see a break in the line, this indicates that the string is going under the mesh. And when there is no break in the line, this indicates the string is going over the mesh.

KNOTS USED IN THE SEWING (BRAIDING) PROCESS

STARTING AND FINISHING KNOT

I will start off with what I call a 'starting and finishing knot', as shown in **Figure 6**. This knot is essentially a double- or triple-sheet bend that has been modified to prevent the knot slipping over the end of a clean mesh, and to ensure it locks itself in position. This knot is used as the name suggests – for starting and finishing off the sewing process.

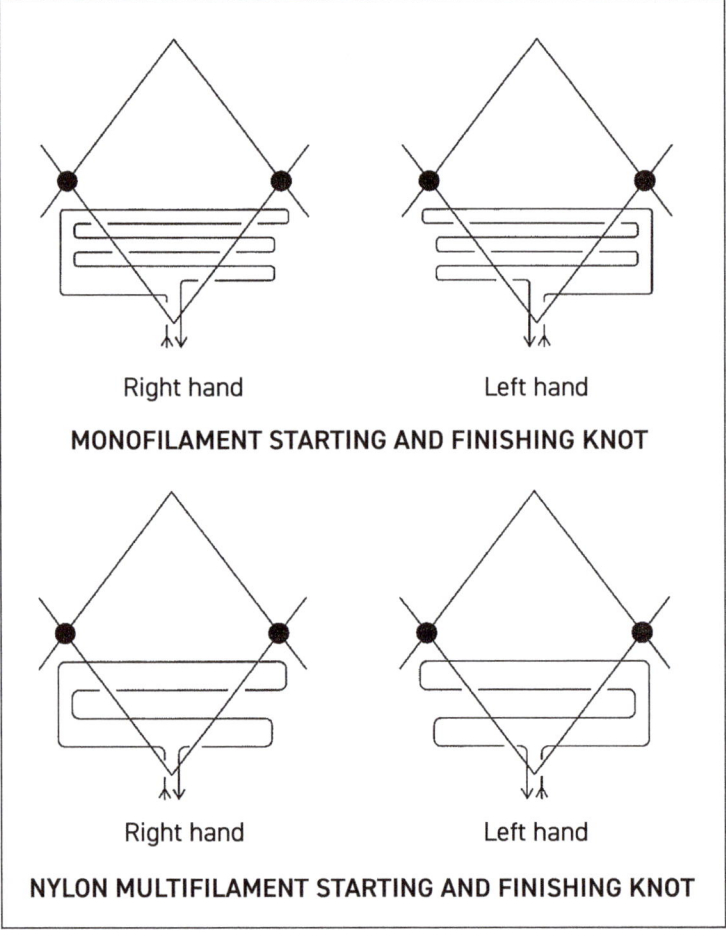

Figure 6

18　MAKING AND MENDING CAST NETS

KNOT USED TO PICK UP TWO MESHES

This knot is used for picking up two meshes at the one time when sewing panels together. It is essentially two half hitches with a locking hitch. Refer to **Figure 6.1**.

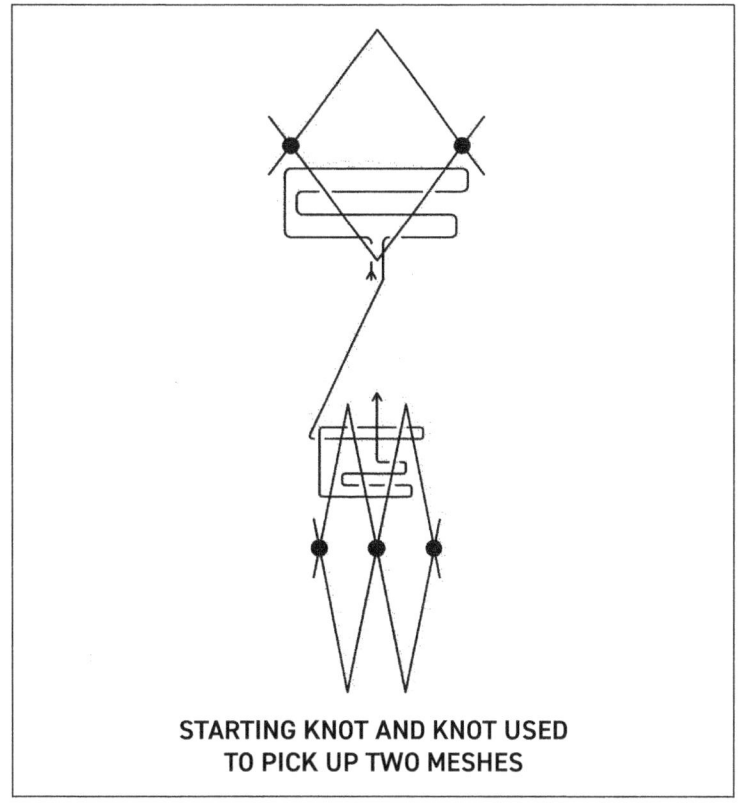

Figure 6.1

SIDE KNOT

This knot is used for sewing two all-points cuts together, and it is a combination of half hitches, as shown in **Figure 6.2**. Throughout this book, I will refer to it as a 'side knot'.

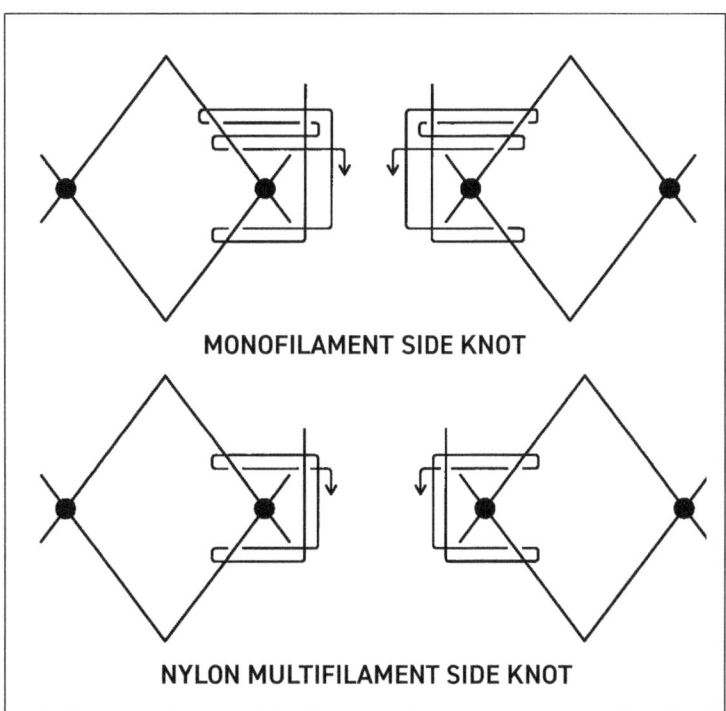

Figure 6.2

FLAT KNOT

The flat knot is used to sew the cleaned meshes together, such as when sewing two panels together, as shown in **Figure 6.3**.

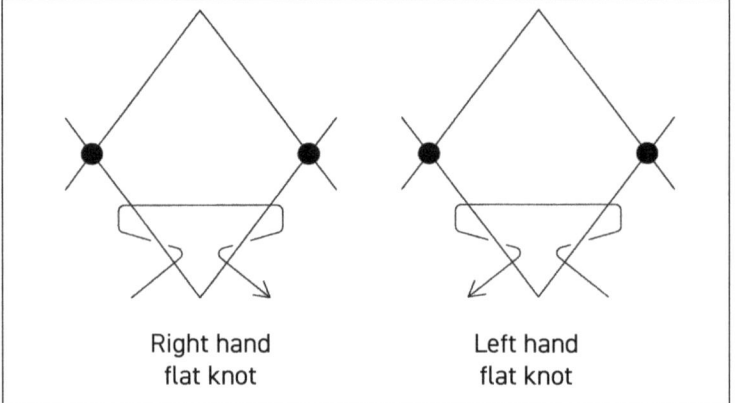

Figure 6.3

CLOVE HITCH WITH A HALF-HITCH LOCK

The clove hitch with a half-hitch lock is used when attaching the lead line to the net. **Figure 6.4** shows two clove hitches with a half-hitch locking knot either side of the lead weight. Note that the half-hitch locks the clove hitch in position, to stop it from loosening.

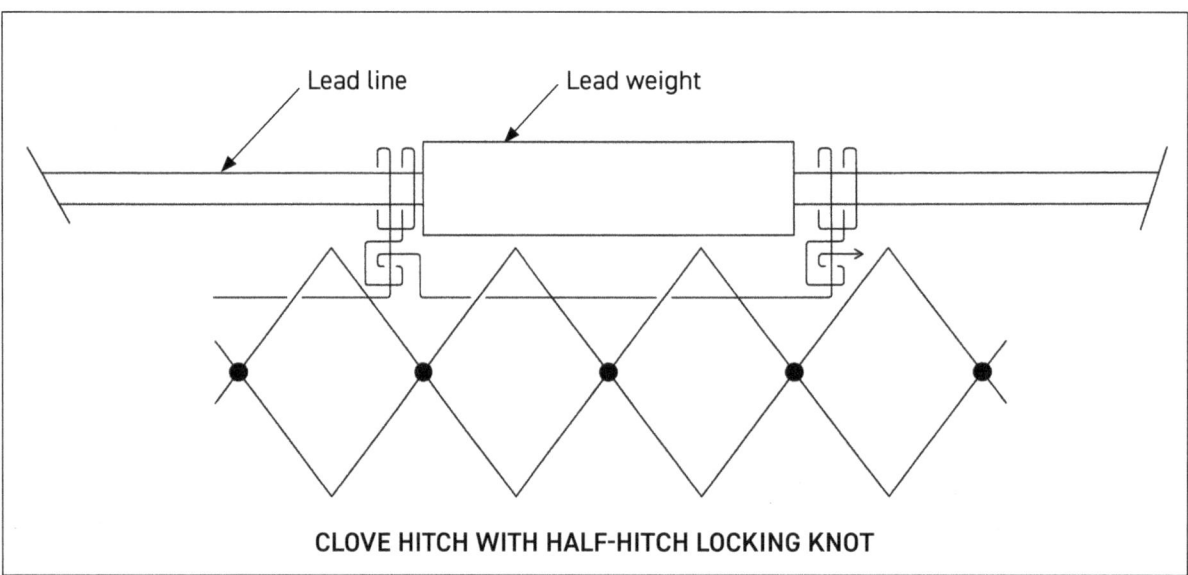

Figure 6.4

SLIPPED HALF KNOT

The slipped half knot is for ease of knot removal. The slipped half knot is used for tying off the waistline, as shown in **Figure 6.5**.

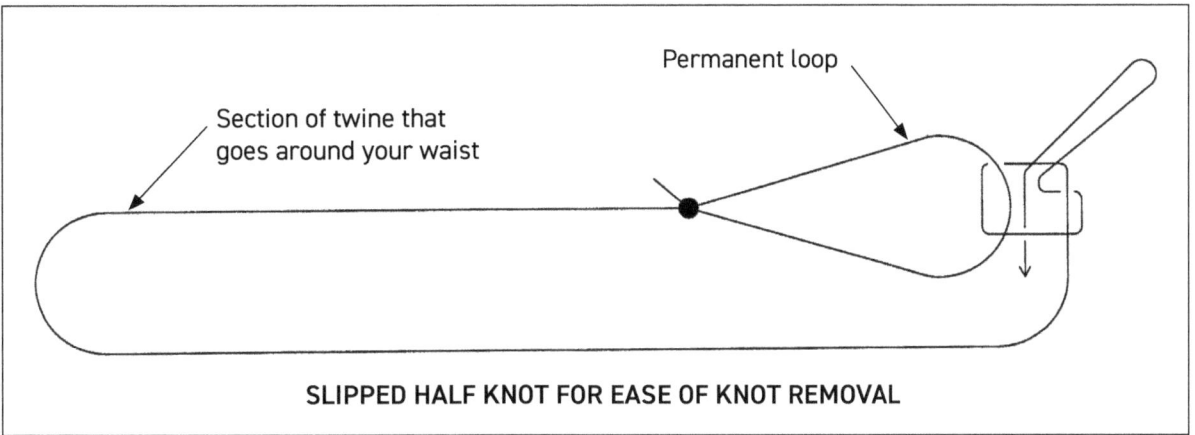

Figure 6.5

SHEET BEND

I would like to include another knot known as a 'sheet bend', which some readers may prefer to use when sewing the cleaned meshes (panels) together. Refer to **Figure 6.6**.

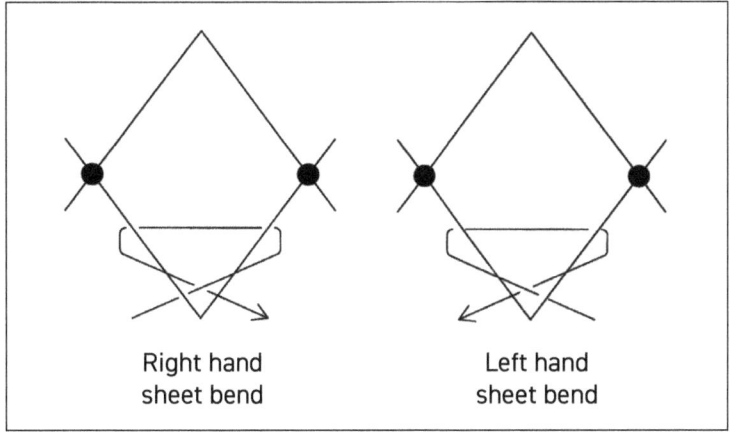

Figure 6.6

FUNDAMENTAL KNOT-TYING TECHNIQUES

The following photos show the fundamental techniques required to tie the above knots. The use of these techniques will become more apparent during the sewing process.

1. Figure 6.7 (a) shows the middle finger under the knot that is ready to be pinched in position.

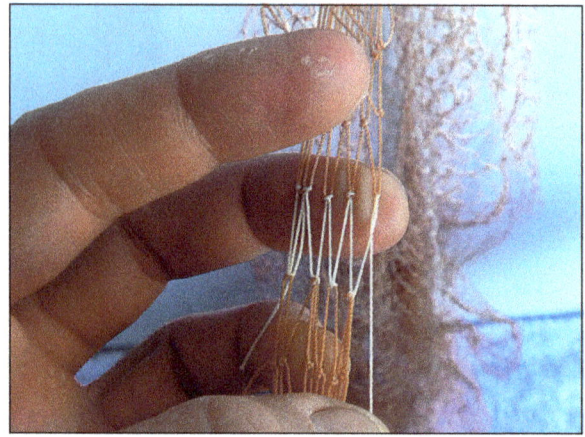

Figure 6.7 (a)

2. Figure 6.7 (b) shows the use of the thumb and the middle finger pinching the knot in position.

Figure 6.7 (b)

3. Figure 6.7 (c) shows the string thrown wide and the use of the pointer finger to hold the string in position.

   NOTE that the pointer finger is generally used when tying off to the top panel.

Figure 6.7 (c)

4. **Figure 6.8 (a)** shows the meshing needle threaded through the mesh while the thrown string is held in position with the pointer finger.

Figure 6.8 (a)

5. **Figure 6.8 (b)** shows the last stages of the knot before it is pulled between the pinched thumb and the middle finger.

Figure 6.8 (b)

6. **Figure 6.8 (c)** shows the completed flat knot.

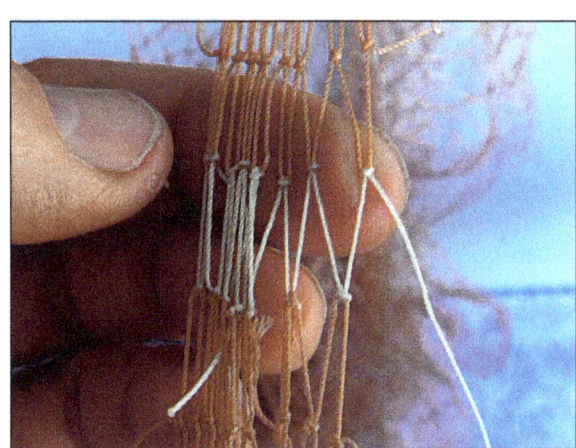

Figure 6.8 (c)

MAKING AND MENDING CAST NETS

7. **Figure 6.9 (a)** shows the use of the little finger to hold the string in position.

   NOTE that the little finger is generally used when tying off to the bottom panel.

Figure 6.9 (a)

SEWING AN ALL-POINTS MESH CUT

Now that you know the knots, let's get to the good part and start constructing your cast net. The process starts by joining the all-points cut of your first panel together. This first step can best be described via a step-by-step process of net construction.

1. This is the stage in which the wall hook and waistline will come into play. Firstly install the wall hook at a level that lies between your belly button and your sternum, while you are in a seated position. Ensure that the hook is fixed into a suitable material so that it doesn't pull out. Even more importantly, make sure that your partner is happy with where you intend on putting a small hole in the wall, otherwise you may get shreds torn off you by a sharp tongue!

2. Place two meshes of the opposing all-points cut on the hook, as shown in **Figure 6.10**. Ensure that there are no twists in the panel prior to sewing the two all-points cuts together.

3. Next, thread the waistline through the last two meshes of the panel, as shown in **Figure 6.10**, and tie off around your waist, adjusting the waistline and your seating position until the meshes between the hook and the waistline are taut. It should now be apparent that the two all-points cuts lie offset to each other.

On larger panels it will be necessary to count down between six and ten meshes and thread the waistline through at that point. This should make for a comfortable sewing length.

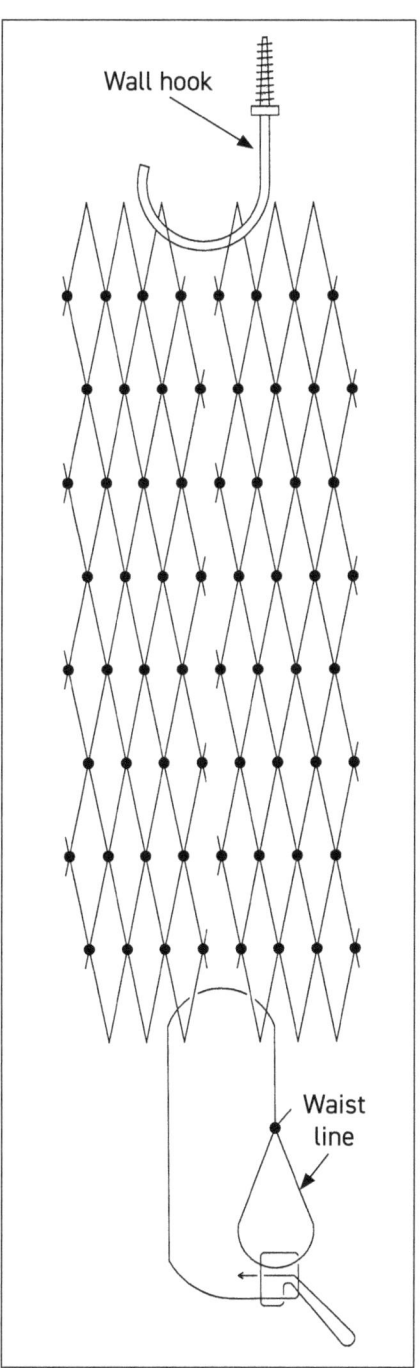

Figure 6.10

4. Now it's time to join the two all-points cuts together. Using the small meshing needle loaded with the 210/6-ply twine (or 5-kg mono line) tie a starting knot, as shown in **Figure 6** (page 18), to the mesh with the single bar cut. Once this is complete, loop the twine over the hook and tie a side knot to the first all-points cut, as shown in **Figure 6.2** (page 19). Continue the process of sewing the all-points cuts together until you reach the last all-points mesh. At this point, you may have needed to shift the position of the meshes on the hook and the waistline a number of times, until you now have the waistline through the very last two meshes, as shown in **Figure 6.10** and **6.11**. Now wrap the twine around the waistline, and using a finishing knot, join it to the mesh with the single bar. **Figure 6.12** shows a photo of the finished join.

The next step is to repeat the above process for the second panel. You will now have two panels that you can sew together.

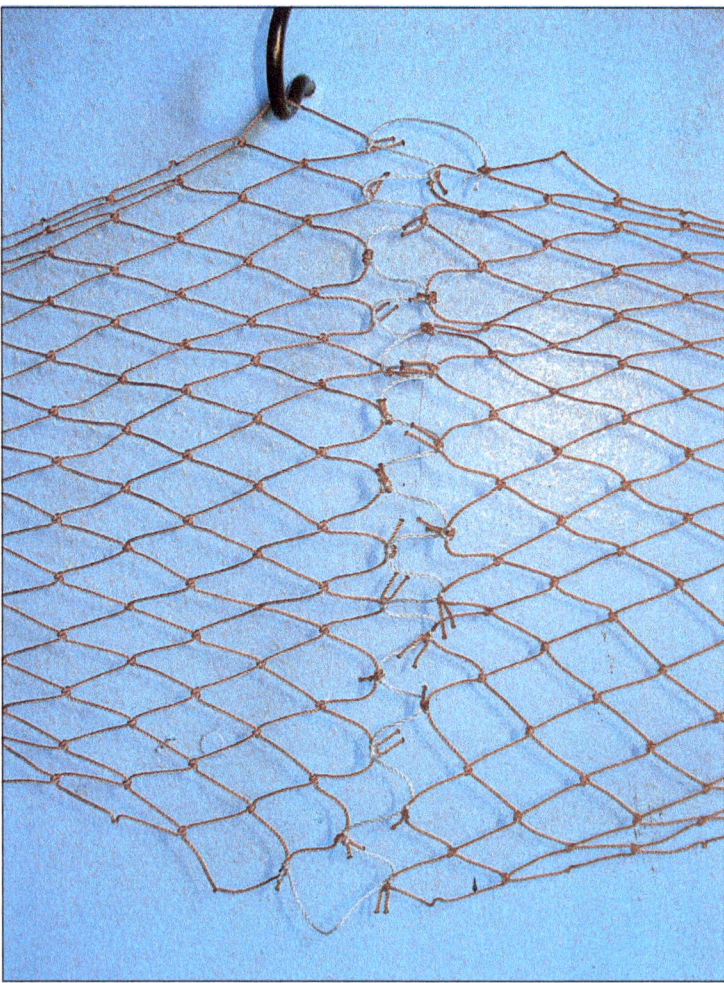

Figure 6.11

Figure 6.12

SEWING AN ALL-CLEANED MESH CUT

This is the point where you sew the two panels together, and again this is best described via a step-by-step process.

1. At this point you will need to attach the swivel to the first panel prior to sewing the two panels together. This process is outlined in Chapter 7. The swivel is then hooked onto the wall hook, as shown in **Figure 6.13**.

2. The next step is to thread the waistline through the second panel. Take the threading tool and loop the waistline in half over the slot in the threading tool. Count down six meshes in the second panel and start threading the waistline through the meshes in the direction of the braid. Refer to **Figure 6.14**. Fill the waistline to a point you are comfortable with – as a starting point I would suggest 150 meshes or more. Pull one-half of the waistline through the meshes and withdraw the threading tool. You should now have the meshes on your waistline. Tie the waistline off around your waist, as shown in **Figure 6.15**. You are now ready to sew the two panels together.

Figure 6.13

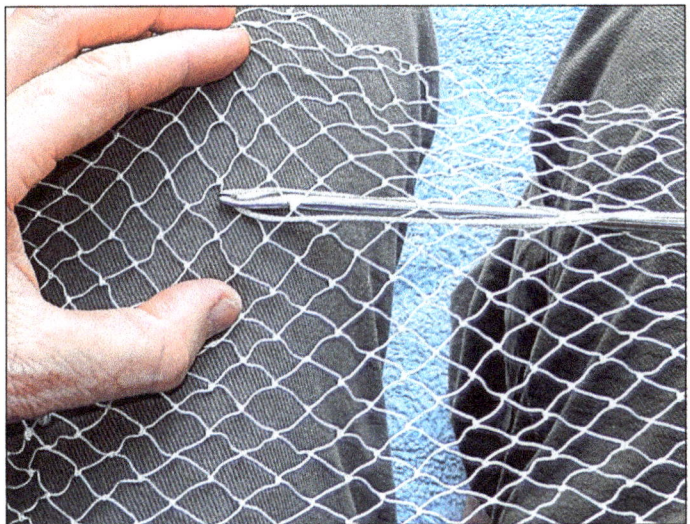

Figure 6.14

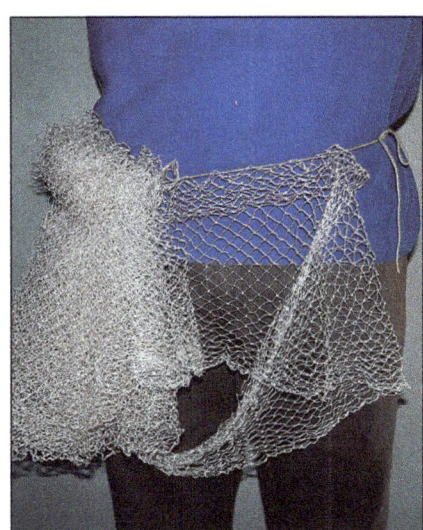

Figure 6.15

MAKING AND MENDING CAST NETS 27

3. Start by taking the small meshing needle loaded with the 210/6-ply twine (or 5-kg mono line) and tie a starting knot on a cleaned mesh on the first panel, as shown in **Figure 6.16**.

4. As the ratio between the first and second panel is 1 is to 2, this means that for every mesh you pick up on the first panel, you will need to pick up two meshes on the second panel. Now pass the meshing needle through two meshes on the second panel and tie off, as shown in **Figure 6.1** (page 19). Note that it is important to set the braid length to equal one-half of the mesh length. Refer to **Figure 6.16**. You may need to adjust your seating position to get this right.

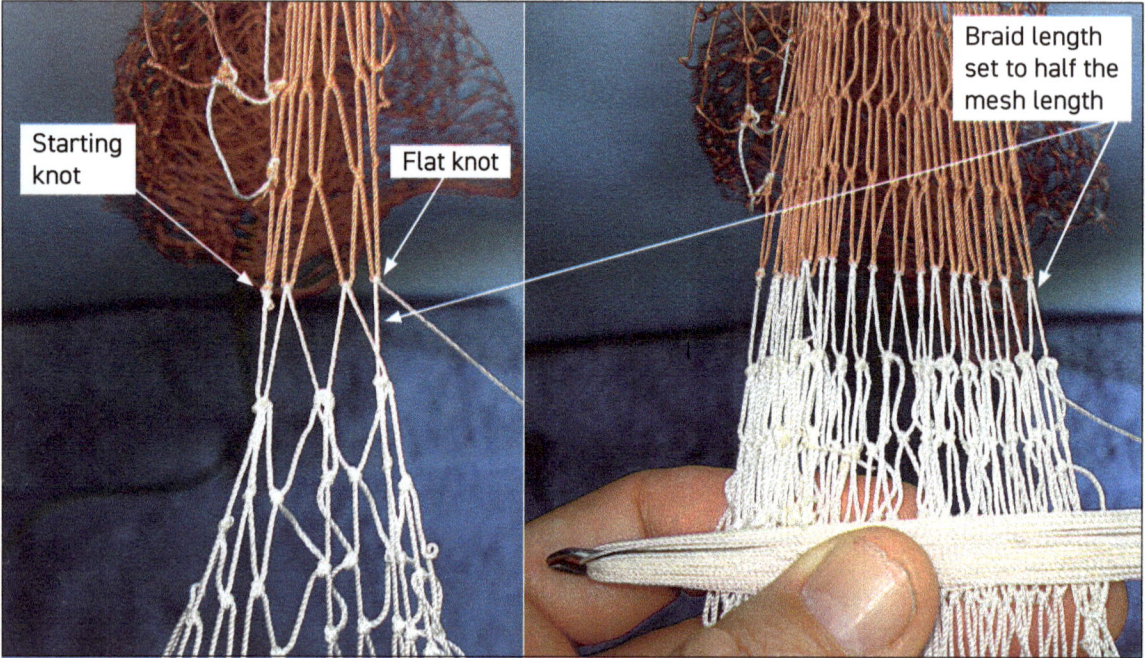

Figure 6.16

5. Pass the meshing needle through a single mesh on the first panel and tie it off with a flat knot, as shown in **Figure 6.3** (page 20), ensuring again to set the braid length. Once set, the braid length should fall naturally into position via the above process.

6. Repeat the above processes until you have completely sewn the first panel to the second panel.

7. Continue to repeat the above process until all of the corresponding panels are sewn together, ensuring to be mindful of the ratios between the panels.

8. **Figure 6.17** shows a typical example of a net that is set between the wall hook and the waistline. Here the first panel has been sewn to the second panel.

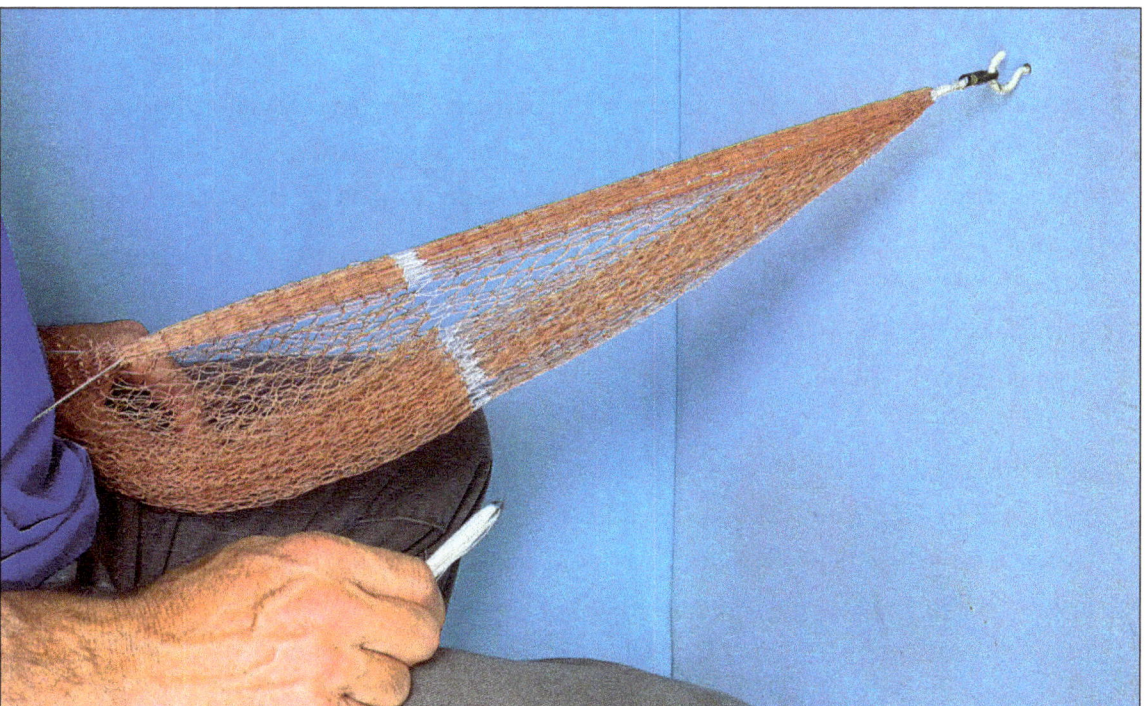

Figure 6.17

7. SWIVEL AND HANDLINE ATTACHMENT

ATTACHING THE SWIVEL TO THE NET

The swivel is attached to the first panel of your cast net along the single or double selvedge edge. The swivel is necessary to prevent the handline from twisting into a knot while you are casting your net. Follow the step-by-step process below, to join the first panel of your cast net to the swivel.

1. Cut a length of 18-ply nylon multifilament twine approximately 1 m long.

2. Fold the twine in half and melt the two free ends together using a lit mosquito coil. The melted ends can be rolled between your fingers to aid in the fusion of the two ends. You will need to let the melted ends cool to a level to prevent your fingers from being burnt but still be pliable enough to allow forming.

3. The looped end is then fed through one eye of the swivel, and the now fused end is fed through the loop and pulled tight onto the swivel. (This is known as a cow hitch.) Refer to **Figure 7**.

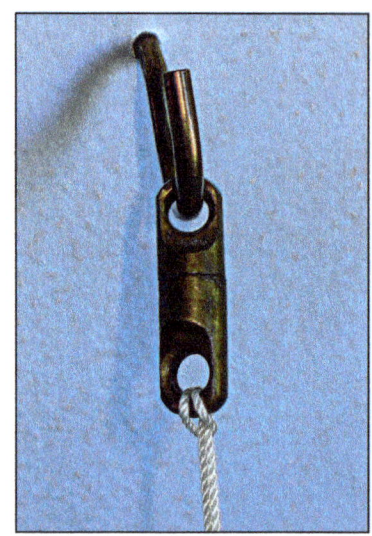

Figure 7

4. Now take the threading tool and loop the waistline in half over the slot in the threading tool. Start threading the waistline through the all-cleaned meshes on one edge of the panel, in the direction of the braid. Pick up half of the meshes and pull one-half of the waistline through the meshes and withdraw the threading tool. You should now have 48 meshes on your waistline, if you are making a multifilament nylon cast net, as shown in **Figure 7.1**. Tie the waistline off around your waist. You are now ready to join the swivel to the first panel of your cast net.

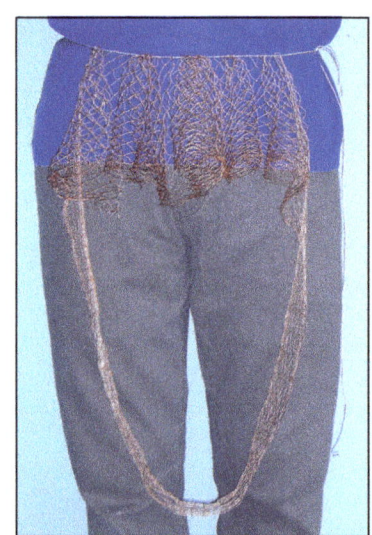

Figure 7.1

5. Hook the free eye of the swivel onto the wall hook, as shown in **Figure 7.2**.

6. Take the free end of the 18-ply twine attached to the swivel, and wrap it over the threading tool. Now pick up 16 meshes (20 meshes for monofilament nets) on the same side that the waistline is attached. Pass the end of the 18-ply twine back through the swivel from the same side that you picked up the meshes on, as shown in **Figure 7.2**.

7. Then pick up another 16 meshes (20 meshes for monofilament nets) on the opposite side not attached to the waistline. Now pass the end of the 18-ply twine back through the swivel from the same side that you picked the meshes up on. Refer to **Figure 7.3**.

Figure 7.2

Figure 7.3

MAKING AND MENDING CAST NETS   31

8. Repeat the process until all the meshes are picked up. Refer to **Figure 7.4**.

9. Ensure that the loop lengths are even and neat, at approximately 25 mm (1 inch) long. Then tie a series of half-hitch knots down around the length of the loops, starting from the base of the swivel to the end of the loops at the top of the cast net. Refer to **Figure 7.5** and **Figure 7.6**.

10. Pull apart the ends of the fused twine, wrapping them separately in opposite directions around the series of half-hitch knots, and tie off with a reef knot. Cut off the excess twine and melt the ends to prevent fraying. Make sure that you don't melt the ends of the twine excessively as to create a catch point for meshes to hook on. Refer to **Figure 7.7** and **Figure 7.8**.

Figure 7.4

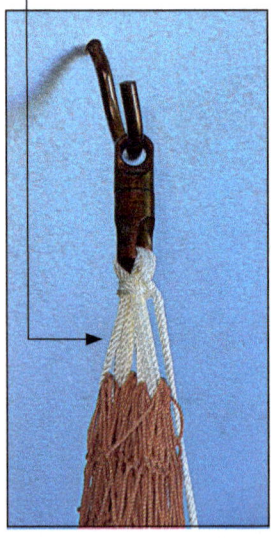

Approximately 25-mm loop length

Figure 7.5

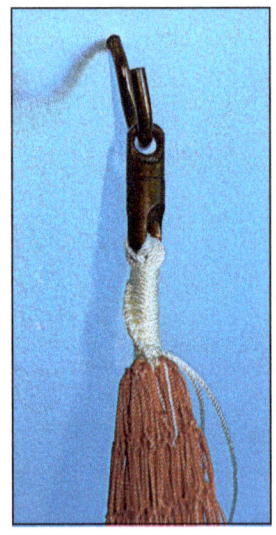

Figure 7.6

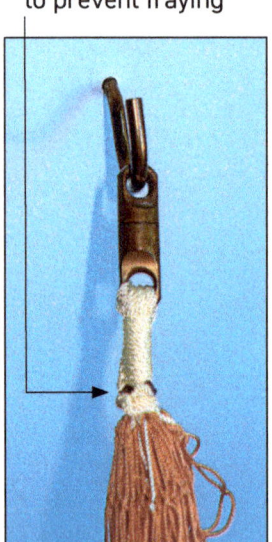

Reef knot with free ends melted to prevent fraying

Figure 7.7

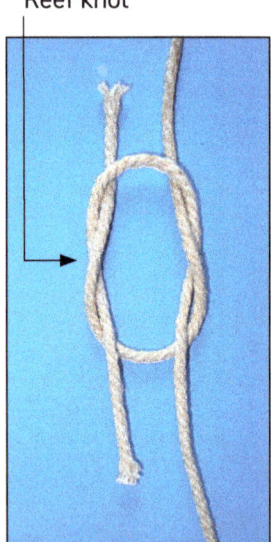

Reef knot

Figure 7.8

32   MAKING AND MENDING CAST NETS

ATTACHING THE HANDLINE TO THE SWIVEL

There are two eye splices that need to be formed: one to form a sliding loop that will secure the handline to your wrist, and one to attach the handline to the swivel. Firstly, I will take you through some basic rope terminology, and then through the step-by-step process of splicing an eye in a rope.

ROPE TERMINOLOGY

LAY
This is the direction of twist in a three-strand rope. Most ropes are right-hand laid, which is the case here. Refer to **Figure 7.9**.

WORKING END
This is the active end of the rope that is used when splicing. Refer to **Figure 7.9**.

STANDING PART
This is the inactive part of the rope during the splicing process. Refer to **Figure 7.9**.

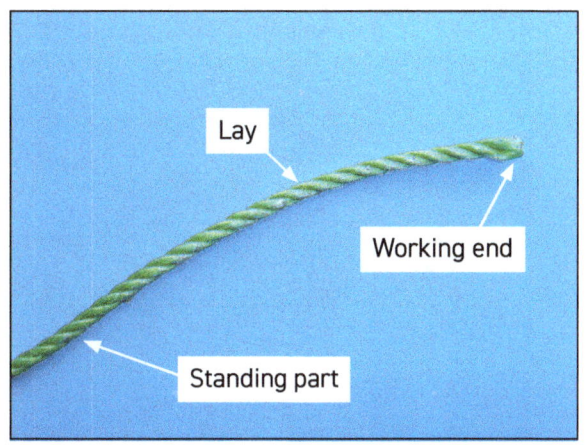

Figure 7.9

SPLICING AN EYE IN A ROPE
The following steps demonstrate how an eye is formed around the standing part of a rope, so as to produce a sliding loop.

1. Unlay the three strands of the 4-mm polypropylene rope to a length of approximately 100 mm (4 inches) long. Refer to **Figure 7.10**. Note that to prevent the ends of each strand from fraying, it is necessary to fuse the ends with a lit mosquito coil that is rubbed against the end of the strand.

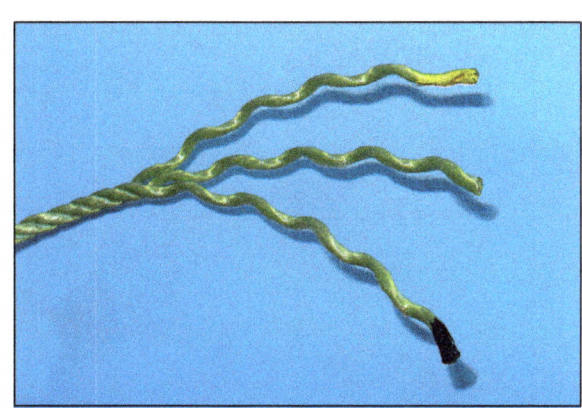

Figure 7.10

2. Form a loop around the standing part of the rope. See **Figure 7.11**. Then take the lowest strand on the working end of the rope and tuck it under the nearest strand on the standing part of the rope. See **Figure 7.11**. **Figure 7.12** shows the process of unlaying a strand on the standing part of the rope, so as to allow the strand on the working end of the rope to be tucked under it.

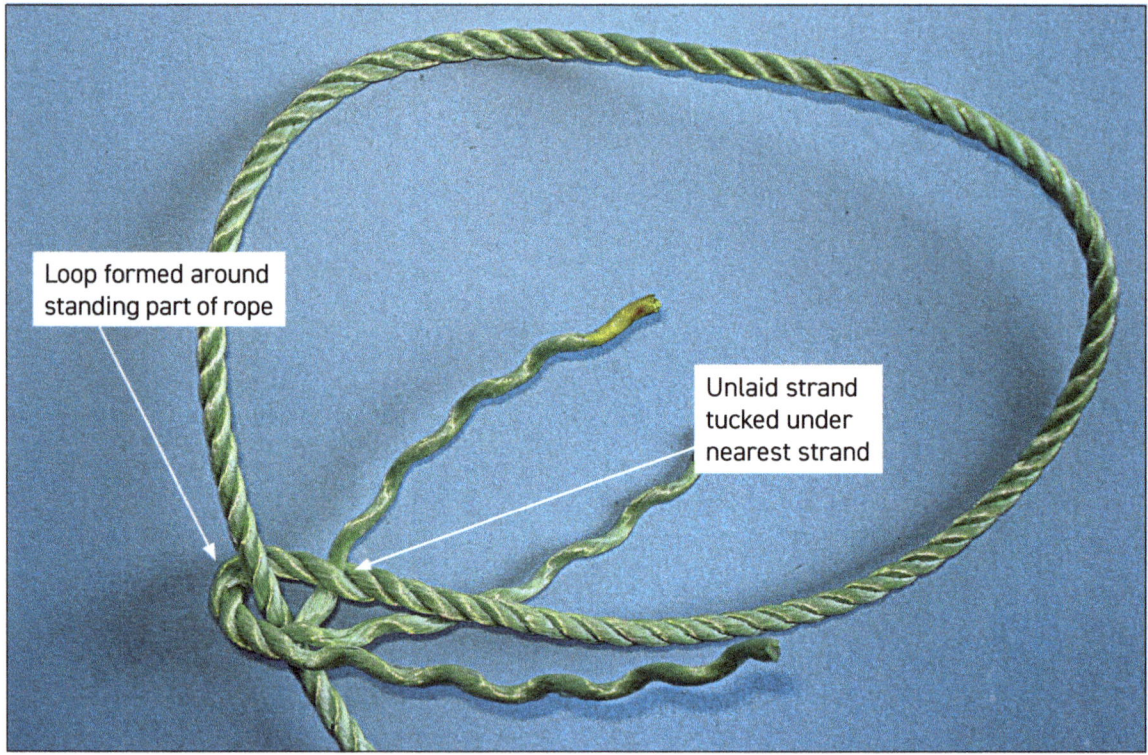

Figure 7.11

Figure 7.12

3. Working against the lay of the rope, separately tuck each of the remaining two unlaid strands under each of the remaining unused strands on the standing part of the rope. The end result should be that shown in **Figure 7.13**. Note that twisting the unlaid strand as you pull it through under the strand on the standing part of the rope will help to bed the strand in and improve the overall appearance of the splice.

Figure 7.13

4. Still working against the lay of the rope, separately tuck each unlaid strand under every second strand on the standing part of the rope. Essentially, you are going over one strand and under the next. **Figure 7.14** shows the highlighted strand going over one strand and under the next. Repeat this process one more time to achieve at least three tucks. Note that at this point, rolling the splice under your foot or between the palms of your hands will again bed the strands in and improve the overall appearance of the splice.

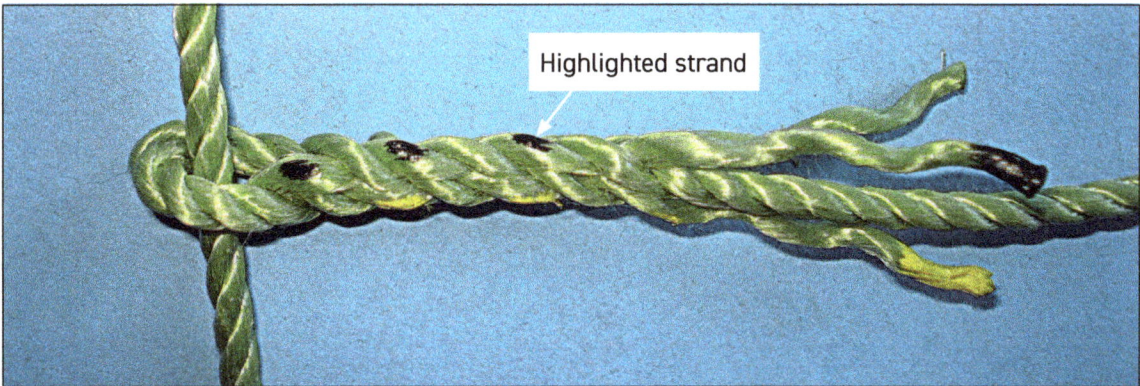

Figure 7.14

MAKING AND MENDING CAST NETS 35

5. Trim and fuse the ends of each unlaid strand flush with the standing part of the rope, ensuring that there are no tags protruding that may catch on the net. This is best achieved by opening up the lay of the rope and melting the free end just back inside of the rope and forming it into the lay of the rope. **Figure 7.15** shows a trimmed strand, and **Figure 7.16** shows the finished sliding loop.

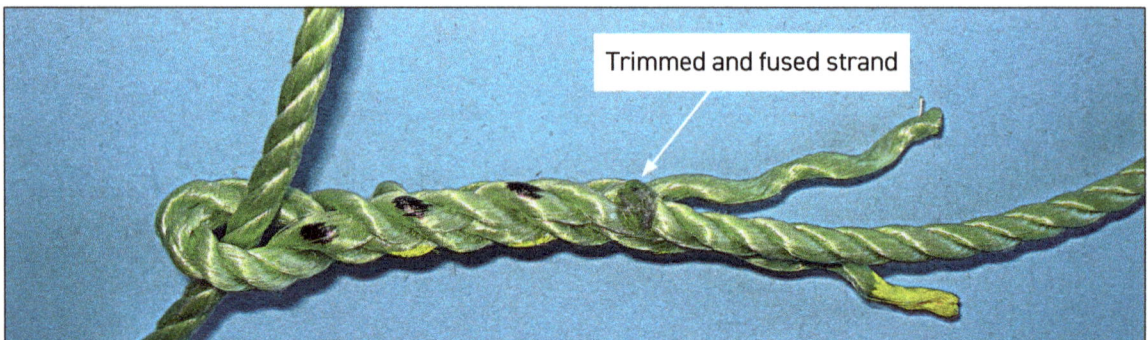

Figure 7.15

Figure 7.16

The process is essentially repeated to attach the handline to the swivel. **Figure 7.17** shows the finished product, with the eye formed through the swivel.

Figure 7.17

8. HANGING THE LEAD LINE

This process involves mounting a series of lead weights and the meshes on the outer circumference of the cast net, to the 2.5-mm diameter venetian blind cord. **Figure 8** shows the standard arrangement for a multifilament cast net, where there are two meshes hung under the lead weight and four in between the two lead weights. This differs from the monofilament arrangement, where you will need to hang three meshes under the lead weight and seven meshes between the lead weights.

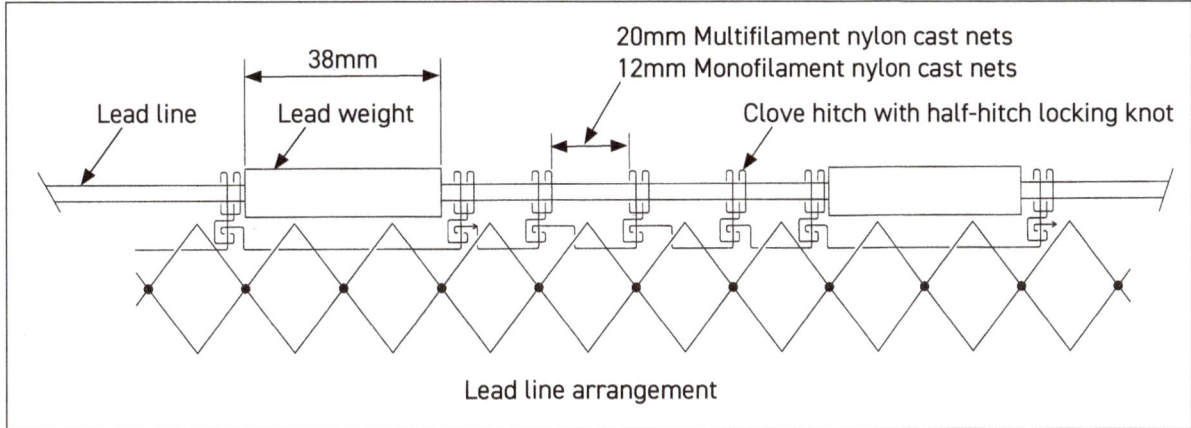

Figure 8

NOTE that in **Figure 8.1**, I have decided to only pick up three meshes between the leads. This decision has come from experience with cast nets that are underweight. You see, a cast net that has more leads or weight (within reason) is generally easier to spread.

In this particular case, the cast net is only small; it was prudent to add a little more weight. For this cast net, it also had the added benefit of dividing into the total number of meshes evenly. In using this method, you can make a net heavier or lighter to suit your individual needs.

Also note that I have placed the double selvedge on the outer circumference of the cast net, as this area receives the most wear and tear.

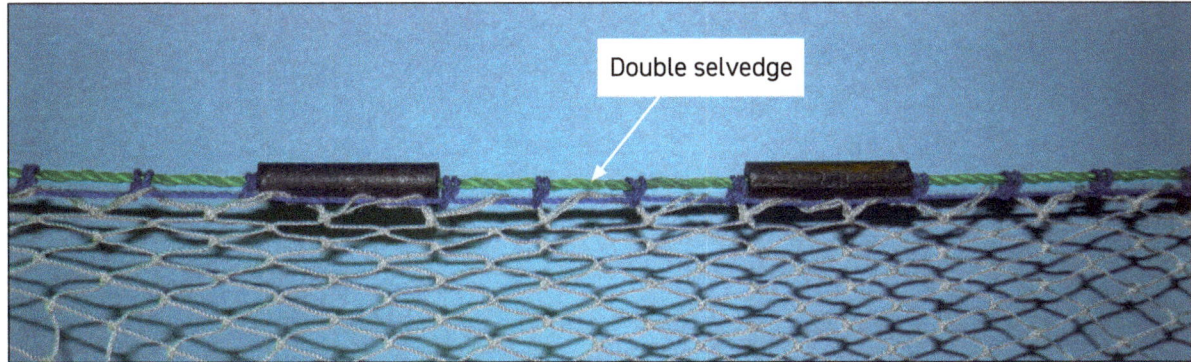

Figure 8.1

I will now take you through a step-by-step process to mount the meshes on the outer circumference of the cast net to the lead line.

1. Thread the required number of leads onto the lead line. Refer to **Figure 8.2**. The required number of leads can be found in Chapter 4 – Net Patterns.

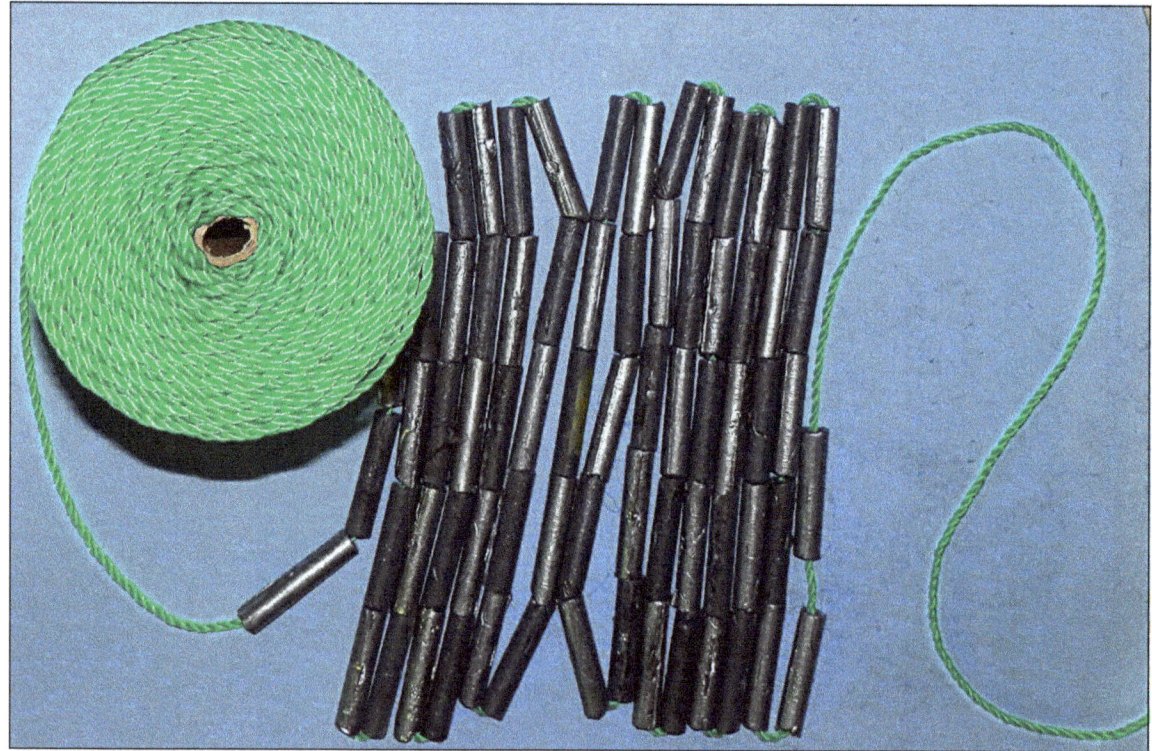

Figure 8.2

2. Tie the lead line taught between two wall hooks, holding 7–8 of the lead weights. Refer to **Figure 8.3**. The distance between the wall hooks should be approximately 2–3 metres (7–10 feet).

One very important step: make sure you're not drilling holes in your wife's favourite section of the wall. I have found that this tends to evoke a barrage of abuse … funny that!

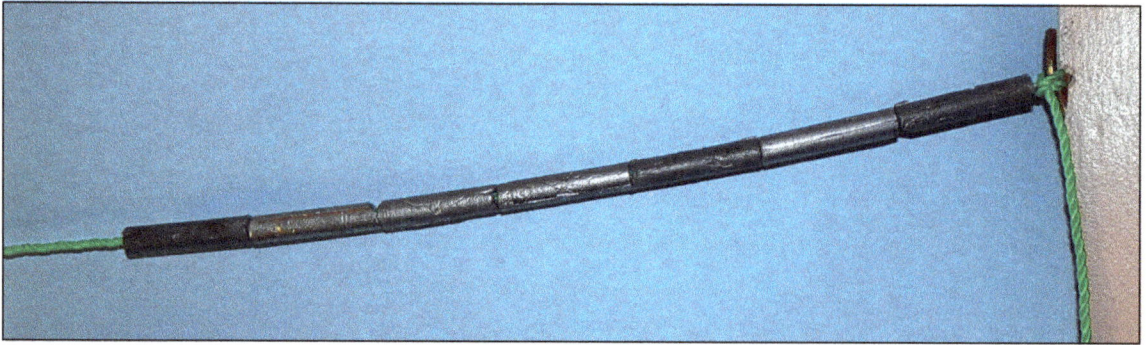

Figure 8.3

3. Using the 210/18-ply twine, tie off to the lead line with a clove hitch and half-hitch locking knot, and then pick up two cleaned meshes on the outer circumference of the cast net and slide a single lead into position. Locate the lead weight in position by tying off on the opposite side of the lead weight, again using the clove hitch and half-hitch locking knot, as shown in **Figure 8**. Note that for a monofilament cast net you will need to pick up three cleaned meshes before sliding the lead weight into position. Also note the 250 mm (10 inch) length of overhang for the lead line and the 210/18-ply twine. This will be used in the finishing off process. See **Figure 8.4**.

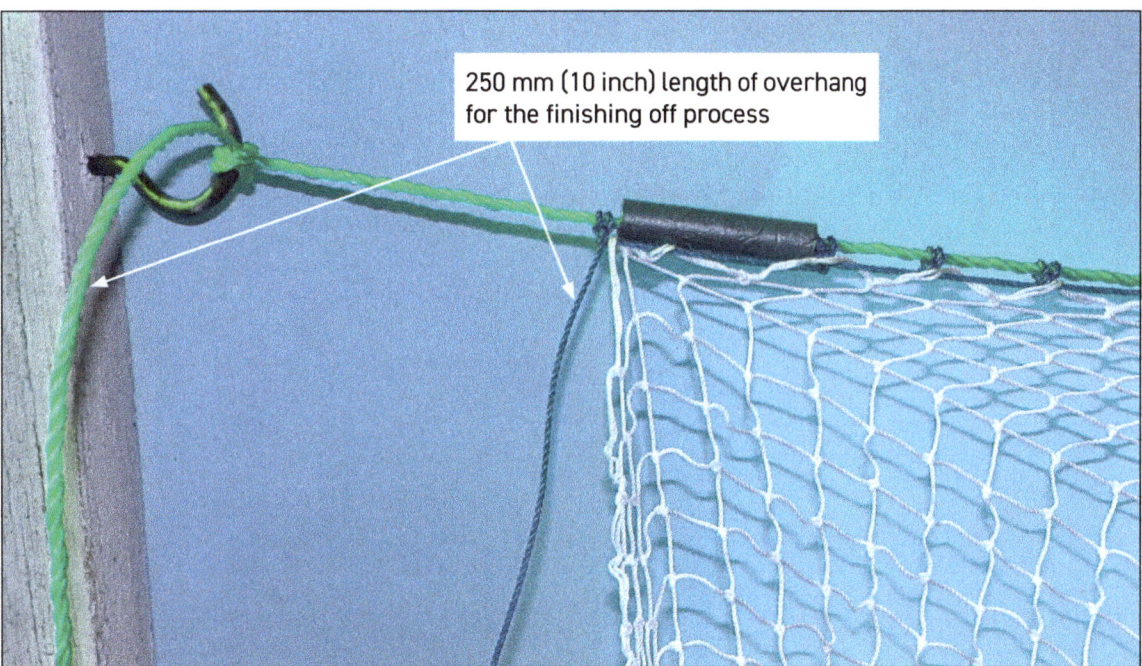

Figure 8.4

4. Pick up a single mesh and tie off to the lead line approximately 20 mm from the last knot formed. Note that 20-mm knot spacing is used for multifilament nylon nets and 12-mm knot spacing for monofilament nets. Continue to repeat this process until you have picked up four meshes, as shown in **Figure 8**. Also note that for monofilament cast nets you will need to pick up seven meshes instead of four.

Now slide another lead weight into position, and repeat the process until you have attached the entire lead line to the outer circumference of the cast net. The spacing between the knots is important, as a narrow spacing will result in the circumference of the lead line being too short, and it will not allow the net to spread out to its full potential. **Figure 8.5** shows a correctly hung lead line that allows the cast net to spread out to its full potential.

Figure 8.5

5. **Finishing off.** At this point you will be down to the last two leads weights, and will need to set the spacing between the lead weights to match that of which you have previously tied. I have found that a few pegs will help hold everything in position during this process. Refer to **Figure 8.6** and **Figure 8.7**.

Now overlap the lead line by using the overhang, and tie off with a clove hitch and half-hitch lock as per normal. Refer to **Figure 8.7**. Continue to hang the lead line, tying the overhang to the main lead line. When you have finished hanging the lead line, cut and join together the 210/18-ply nylon twine with a reef knot. Cut off any excess material and fuse the end on both the lead line and the 210/18-ply nylon twine by using a lit mosquito coil. The end result should look as shown in **Figure 8.8**.

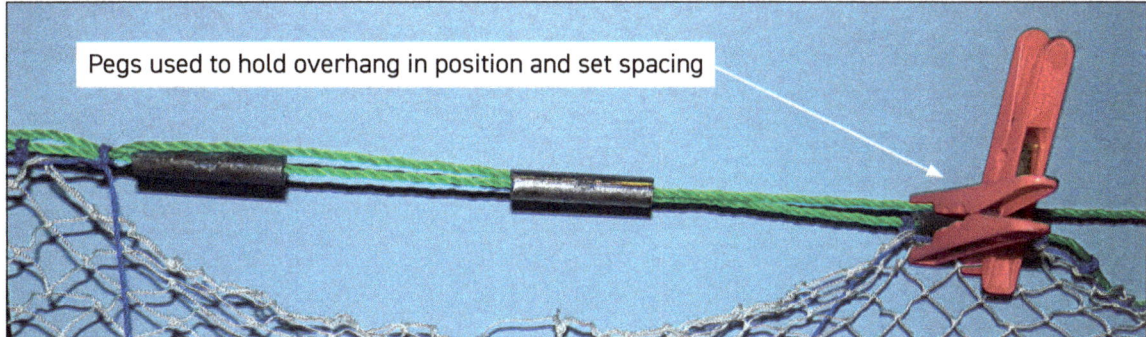

Figure 8.6

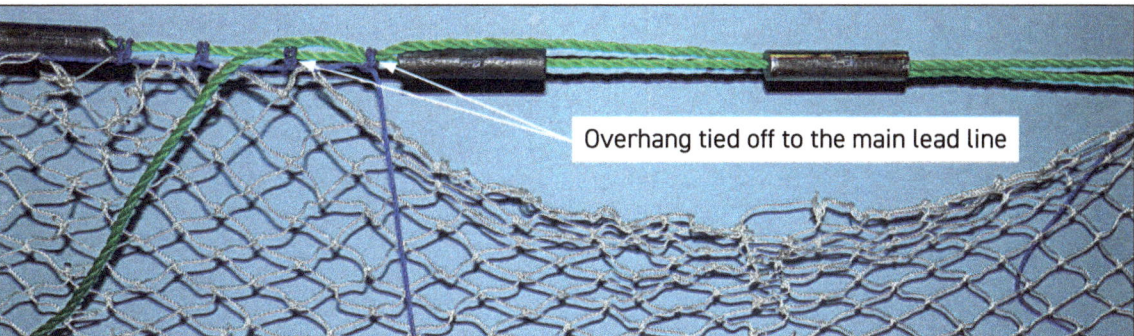

Figure 8.7

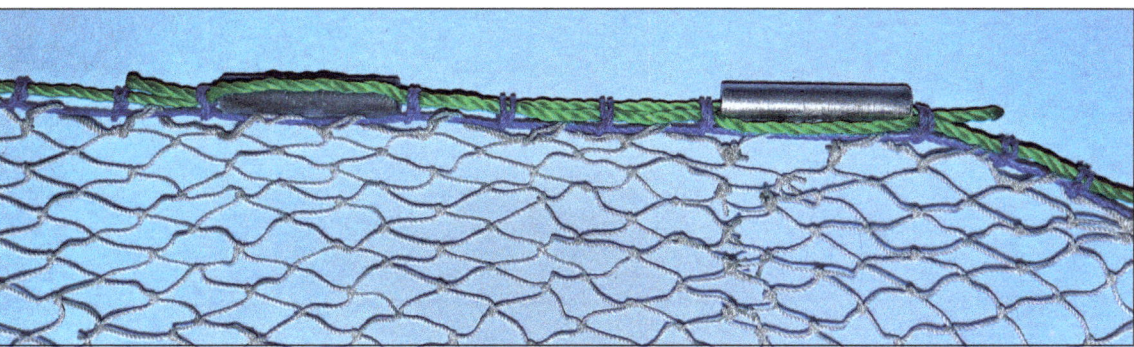

Figure 8.8

MAKING AND MENDING CAST NETS

9. FORMING POCKETS

Pockets are produced by hemming the outer edge of the cast net at individual points. They are formed on the inside of the cast net to aid in the capture of fish. Follow the step-by-step process below to hang your first pocket.

1. Turn the cast net inside out.

2. Select the overlap on the lead line as a starting point – the reason for this is to further strengthen this joint.

3. Select the centre between the two lead weights and count up 14 meshes, as shown in **Figure 9**. Now tie off with a starting knot and a half-hitch knot, as shown in **Figure 9.1** and **Figure 9.2**.

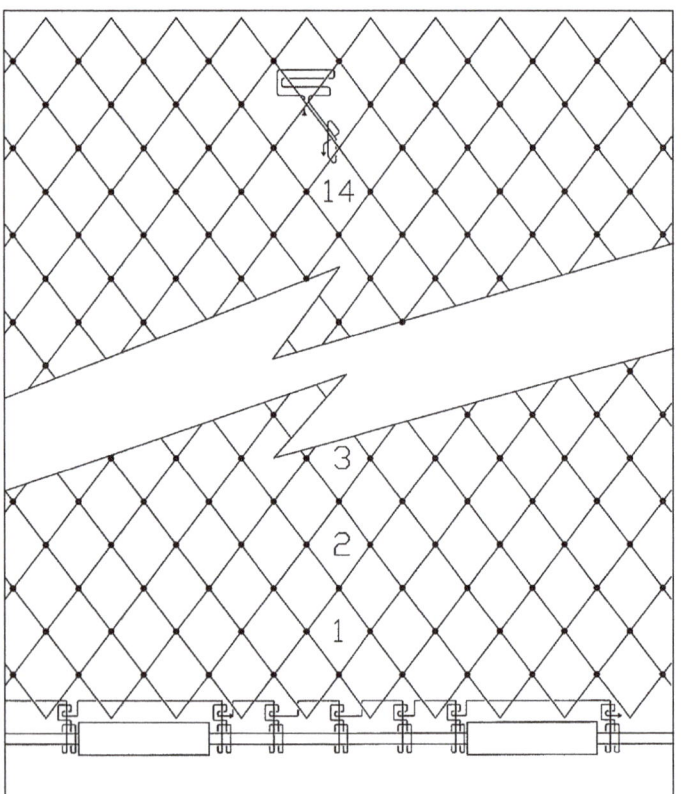

Figure 9

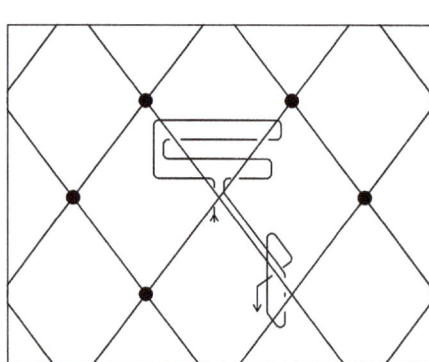

Figure 9.1

Figure 9.2

42   MAKING AND MENDING CAST NETS

4. Pick up the lead line and tie it off, as shown in **Figure 9.3** and **Figure 9.4**, using a clove hitch with a half-hitch locking knot. Take note that the hang length is approximately 25 mm (1 inch) long.

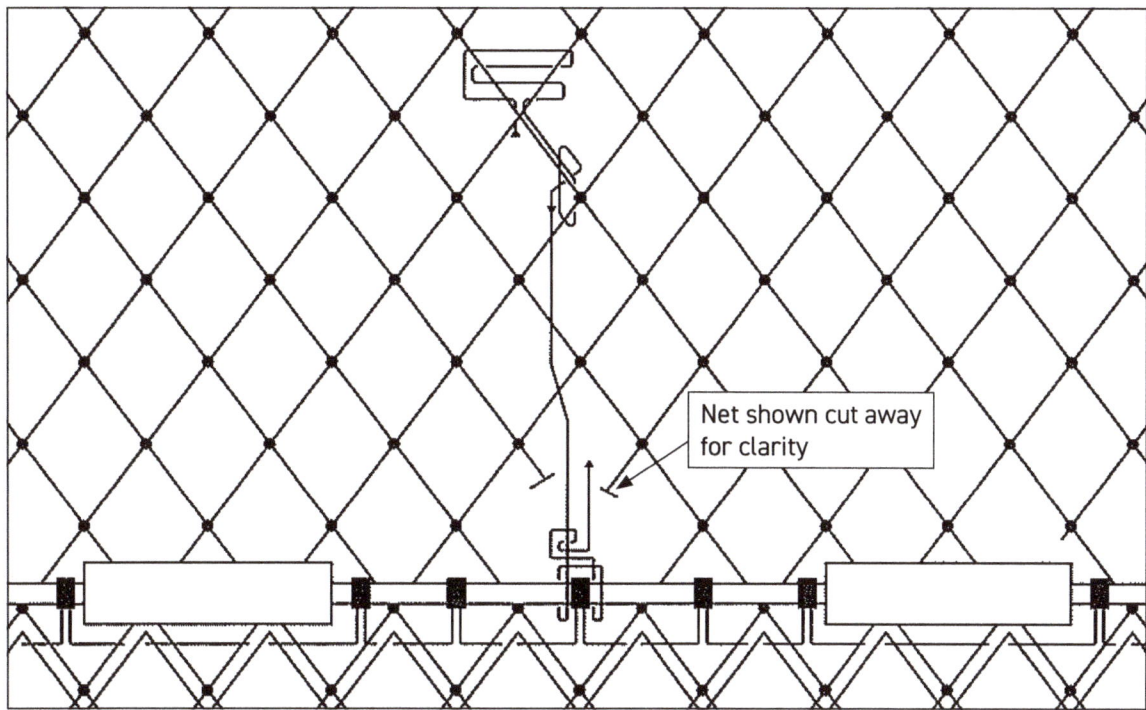

Figure 9.3

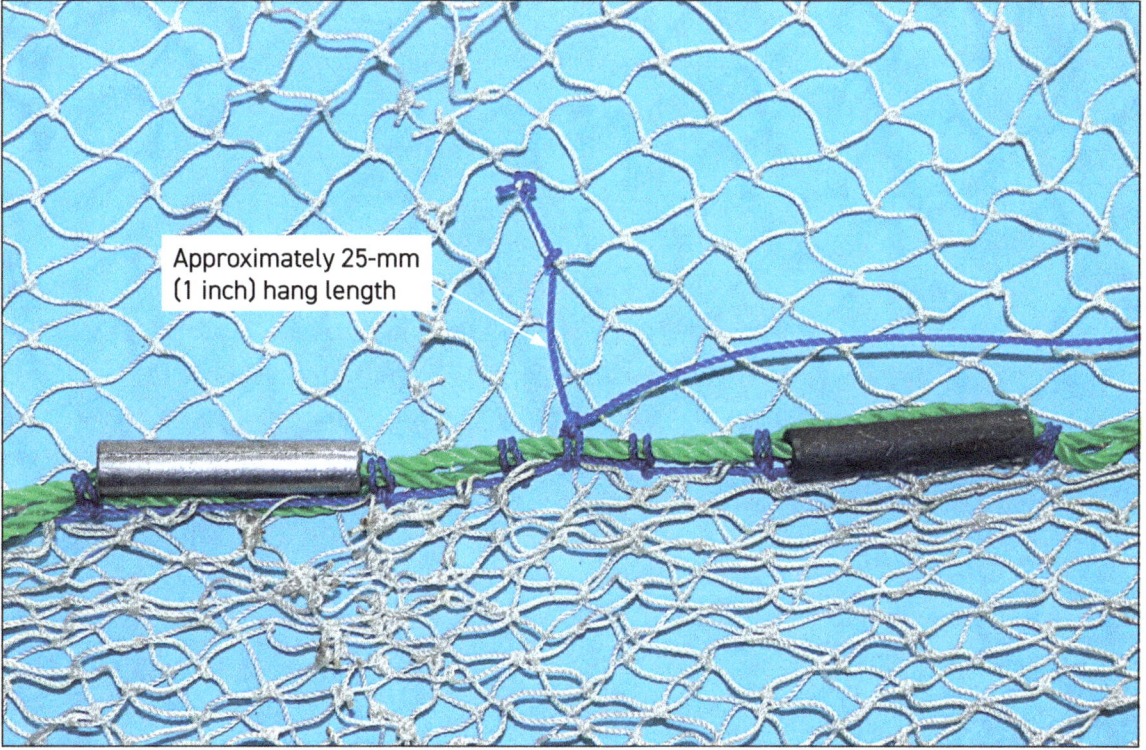

Figure 9.4

MAKING AND MENDING CAST NETS 43

5. All that remains is to finish tying off, as shown in **Figure 9.5** and **Figure 9.6**, using a half-hitch and finishing knot. Note that I have found it easier to use a lit mosquito coil to cut and seal the twine during this process. You will now have formed your first pocket in the cast net.

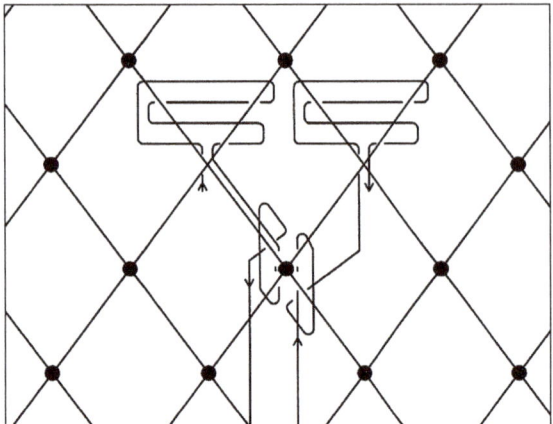

Figure 9.5

Figure 9.6

6. Continue hanging a pocket after every second lead around the entire circumference of the net.

7. Turn the net back around to the right way, and then you are finished!

I have just shown you a typical cast net pocket, and while they all serve the same purpose, you can change the pocket to suit your particular requirements. For example, you can make the pocket deeper so that it will hold larger fish or a greater quantity of smaller fish.

This is done by simply counting up a greater number of meshes and then tying off, as shown above. You can also have a greater hang length, which tends to allow the pockets to open up more and make it easier to remove prawns and bait. For example, you could count up 18 meshes and have a hang length of approximately 75 mm (3 inches). I use this particular style on my monofilament casts nets. Refer to **Figure 9.7**.

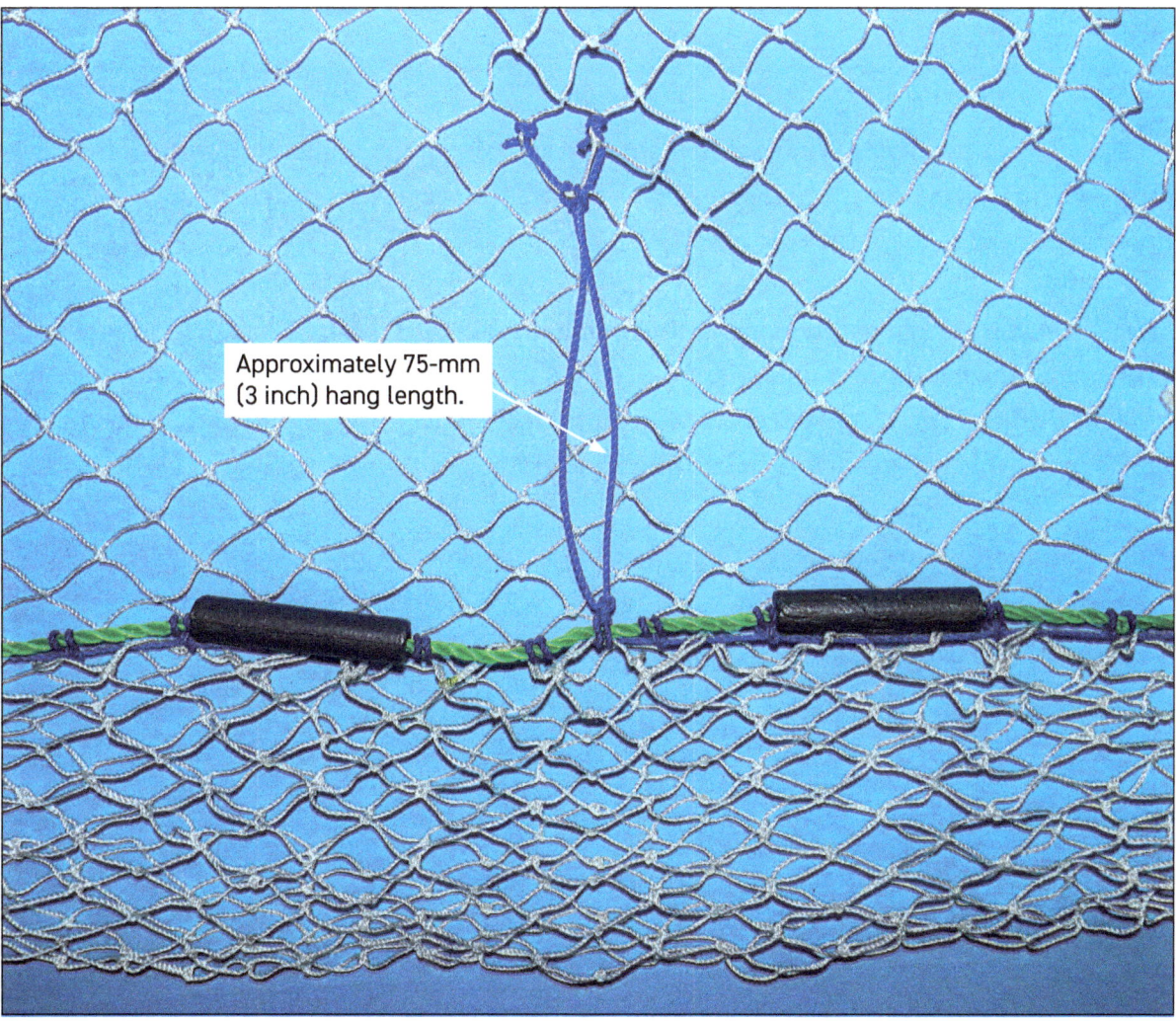

Figure 9.7

Congratulations, you have just completed your cast net.

I have always found a great sense of achievement and satisfaction on finishing a cast net, and I hope you will too. Now it's time to get out there and have some fun casting and catching all those fish. Enjoy!

10. CASTING TECHNIQUES

I will show you two styles of casting nets that I personally use. The first technique is one that I use for larger nets from 12-foot spread and up, and the second technique is one that I use for smaller nets up to 12-foot spread.

Whatever style you choose, remember that practice makes perfect, so don't despair if you can't spread the net the first time. Keep practising, making small alterations to your casting style until you can get the net to spread in that perfect circle. I have found that practising in the backyard on clear ground to be the best spot to start.

The descriptions following are for right-handed people. For left-handers, simply follow the process with the opposite hand.

TECHNIQUE ONE

1. Place the looped end of the handline around your left wrist and loop the handline into the palm of your left hand, as shown in **Figure 10**.

2. Continue to loop the net into your hand and grip the net at a height between your waist and sternum, as shown in **Figure 10.1**.

Figure 10

Figure 10.1

MAKING AND MENDING CAST NETS

3. Using your right hand, pick up one-eighth to one-quarter of the net closest to your body, and place it on your left elbow, as shown in **Figure 10.2** and **Figure 10.3**.

Figure 10.2

Figure 10.3

4. Again, using your right hand, pick up another one-third to one-half of the net that is furthest away from your body, but this time pick up the lead line so that the net opens up, as shown in **Figure 10.4** and **Figure 10.5**.

Figure 10.4

Figure 10.5

5. While still holding a third to half of the net in your right hand, reach around to the back of the net and pick up the remaining net with your right hand, and place it in your left hand, as shown in **Figures 10.6, 10.7, 10.8** and **10.9**.

Figure 10.6

Figure 10.7

Figure 10.8

Figure 10.9

MAKING AND MENDING CAST NETS   49

6. You now have a balanced net ready to cast/throw. Take a step forward with your right foot so that it becomes your leading foot. Now turn side-on so that your right shoulder is pointing approximately in the direction in which you intend to cast. Draw the net back in an anticlockwise motion with your arms and by twisting your hips and upper torso. In a clockwise motion twist your upper torso and hips, following through with your arms, and release the net when you have twisted through an angle of approximately 90–180 degrees. Refer to **Figures 10.10, 10.11** and **10.12**.

Figure 10.10

Figure 10.11

Figure 10.12

TECHNIQUE TWO

1. Place the looped end of the handline around your right wrist and loop the handline into the palm of your right hand, as shown in **Figure 10.13**.

2. Continue to loop the net into your hand and grip the net at your waist height, as shown in **Figure 10.14**.

Figure 10.13

Figure 10.14

MAKING AND MENDING CAST NETS   51

3. Using your left hand, pick up the lead line and place it in your right hand, as shown in **Figure 10.15** and **Figure 10.16**.

Figure 10.15

Figure 10.16

4. Using your left hand, pick up a third of the net that is furthest away from your body, and place it in your right hand, as shown in **Figures 10.17**, **10.18** and **10.19**.

Figure 10.17

Figure 10.18

Figure 10.19

5. Using your left hand, pick up one third of the net closest to your body and remain holding it in your left hand, as shown in **Figure 10.20**.

Figure 10.20

6. You now have a balanced net ready to cast/throw. Take a step forward with your left foot so that it becomes your leading foot. Now turn side-on so that your left shoulder is pointing approximately in the direction in which you intend to cast. Draw the net back in a clockwise motion with your arms and by twisting your hips and upper torso. In an anticlockwise motion twist your upper torso and hips, following through with your arms, and release the net when you have twisted through an angle of approximately 90–180 degrees, as shown in **Figures 10.21**, **10.22** and **10.23**.

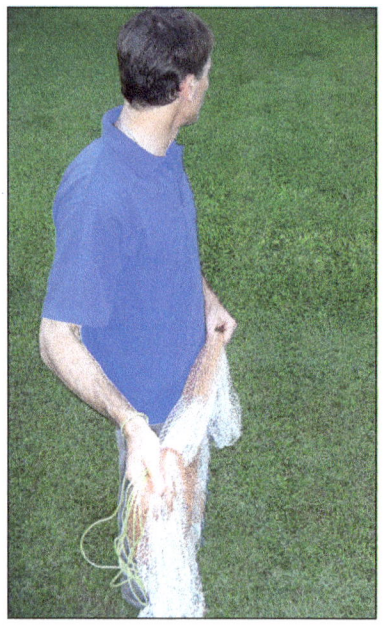
Figure 10.21

Figure 10.22

Figure 10.23

11. MENDING CAST NETS

Throughout your time using a cast net, you will inadvertently tear the net on timber or rock snags in the water, or cast your net over large fish (such as barramundi) that leave your net looking like Swiss cheese after they bust through it. It is very exciting when the latter happens, but your net is left in a terrible state that will require repair.

I will show you the quickest and easiest way to repair those large tears and end up with a professional-looking job that will make it hard to pick where the repair is. And I will show you some of the more simple repairs for those smaller tears.

NOTE that if you have jumped straight to this chapter, you will need to refer to Chapters 1, 2, 3, 5 and 6 to understand the terminology, and the cutting and sewing process.

TRIMMING THE TEAR

This is the first essential step that is required before mending can take place. The tear has to be cleaned to eliminate any unnecessary bars and meshes that may interfere with the continuous remaking of the missing meshes.

When this operation is performed correctly, the trimmed tear will only consist of clean meshes, points and two bars. The two bars are essential for the start and finish of the repair. During the trimming process, you may come across other unwanted bars, and it will be necessary to trim these to make a clean mesh or a points mesh. **Figure 11** shows a tear trimmed ready for mending. Now, before I show you how to mend the tear in **Figure 11**, I will show you how to mend some of the more simple tears first.

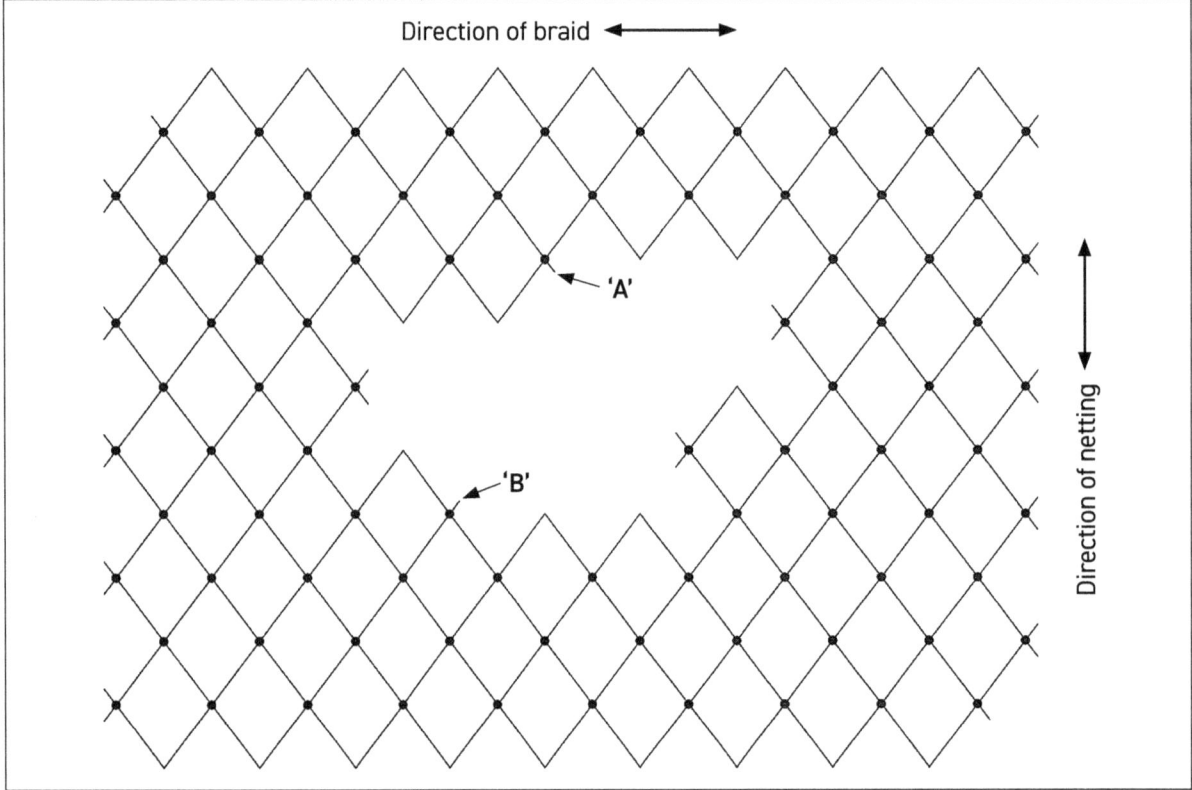

Figure 11

56   MAKING AND MENDING CAST NETS

HORIZONTAL TEAR

Figure 11.1 shows a simple horizontal tear that has been trimmed ready to sew in the missing half mesh or row. Using a wall hook and waistline to set the braid length, sew in the missing half meshes, starting at **'A'** and finishing at **'B'**. **Figure 11.2** shows the half mesh sewn in. This is very similar to joining two panels together, as previously shown in Chapter 6 – Sewing, **Figure 6.16**. The process of using the wall hook and waistline is outlined in **Figure 11.8** of this chapter.

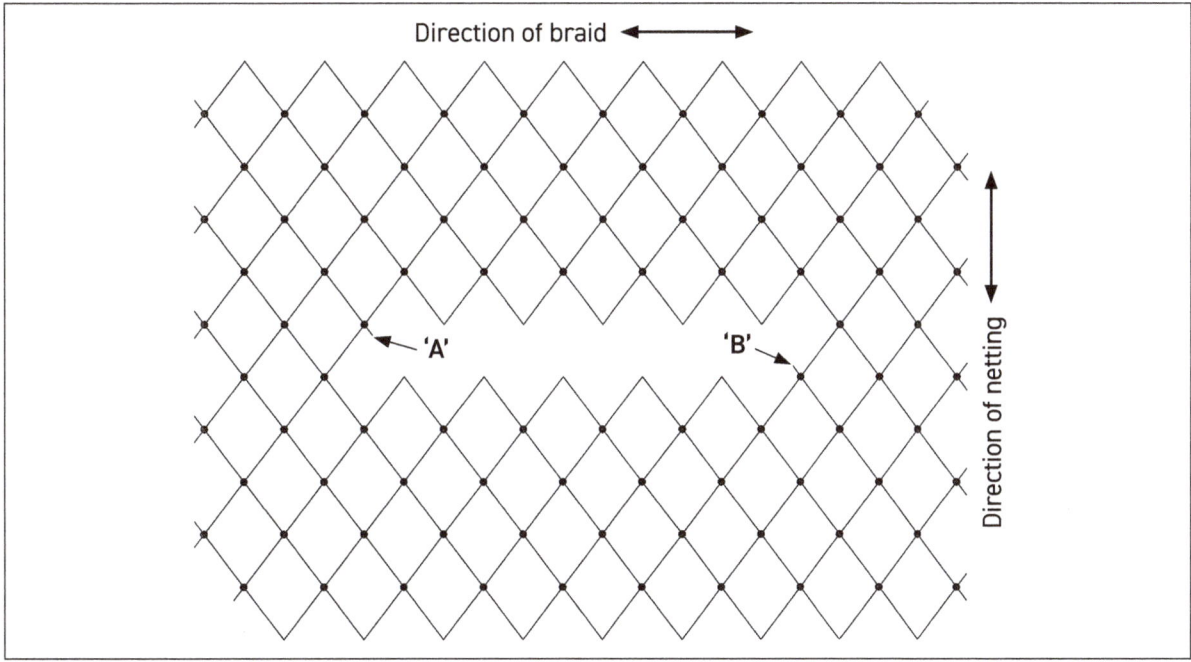

Figure 11.1

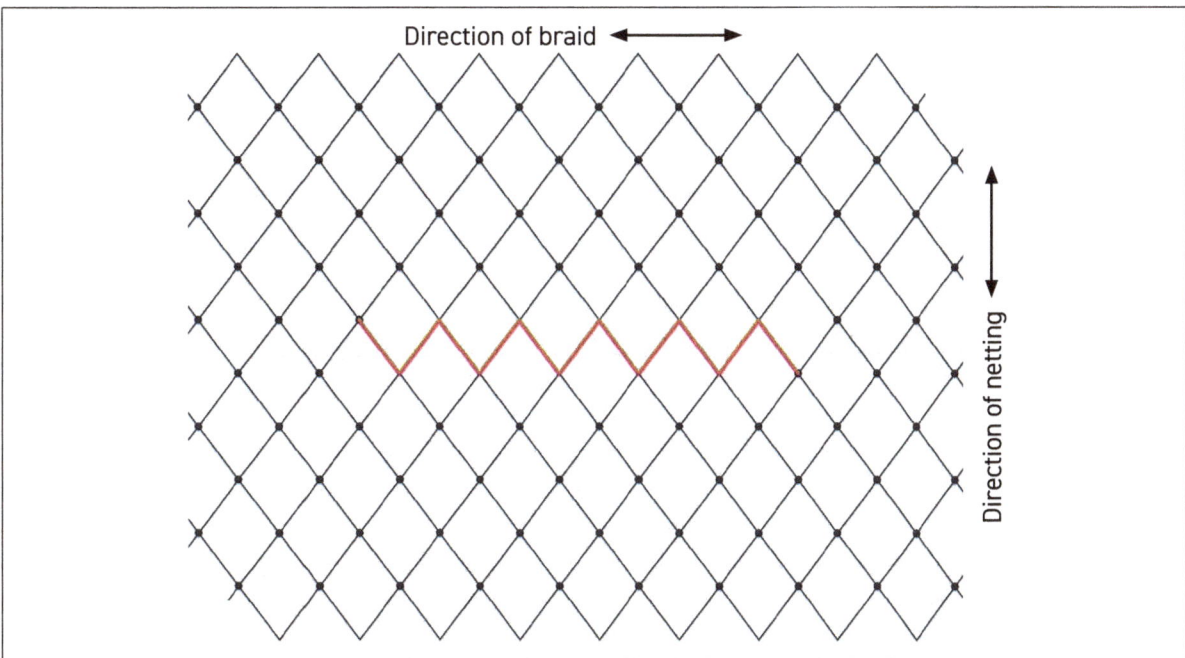

Figure 11.2

VERTICAL TEAR

Figure 11.3 shows a simple vertical tear that has been trimmed ready to sew in the missing half mesh. Using a wall hook and waistline to set the braid length, sew in the missing half meshes, starting at **'A'** and finishing at **'B'**. **Figure 11.4** shows the half mesh sewn in. This is very similar to joining the ends of a panel together, as previously shown in Chapter 6 – Sewing, **Figure 6.11**.

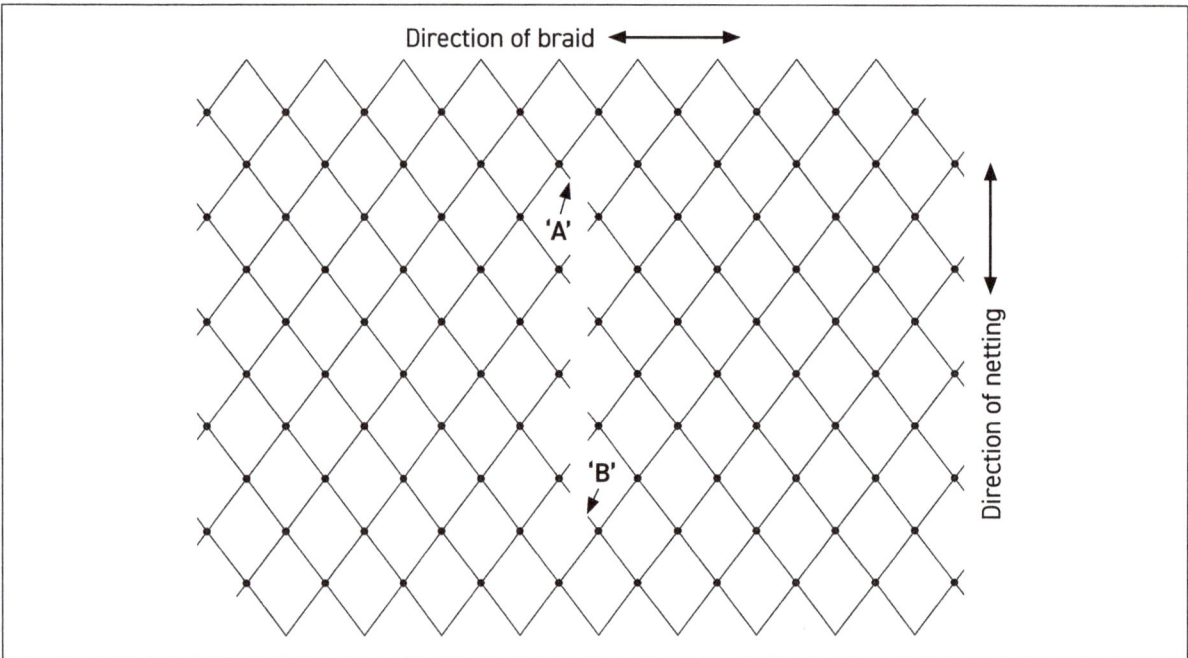

Figure 11.3

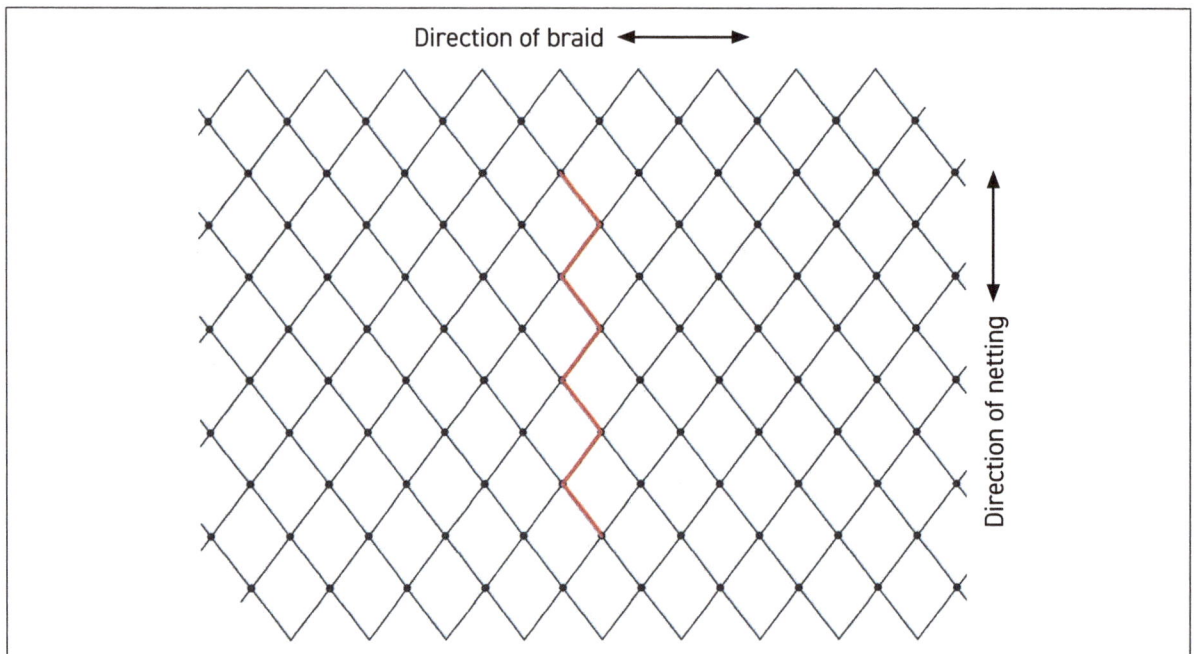

Figure 11.4

OBLIQUE TEAR

Figure 11.5 shows a simple oblique tear that has been trimmed ready to sew in the missing half mesh. Again using a wall hook and waistline to set the braid length, sew in the missing half meshes, starting at **'A'** and finishing at **'B'**. The process of using the wall hook and waistline is outlined in **Figure 11.8** of this chapter. Note that the mending technique used here is a combination of the horizontal and vertical tear. **Figure 11.6** shows the half mesh sewn in.

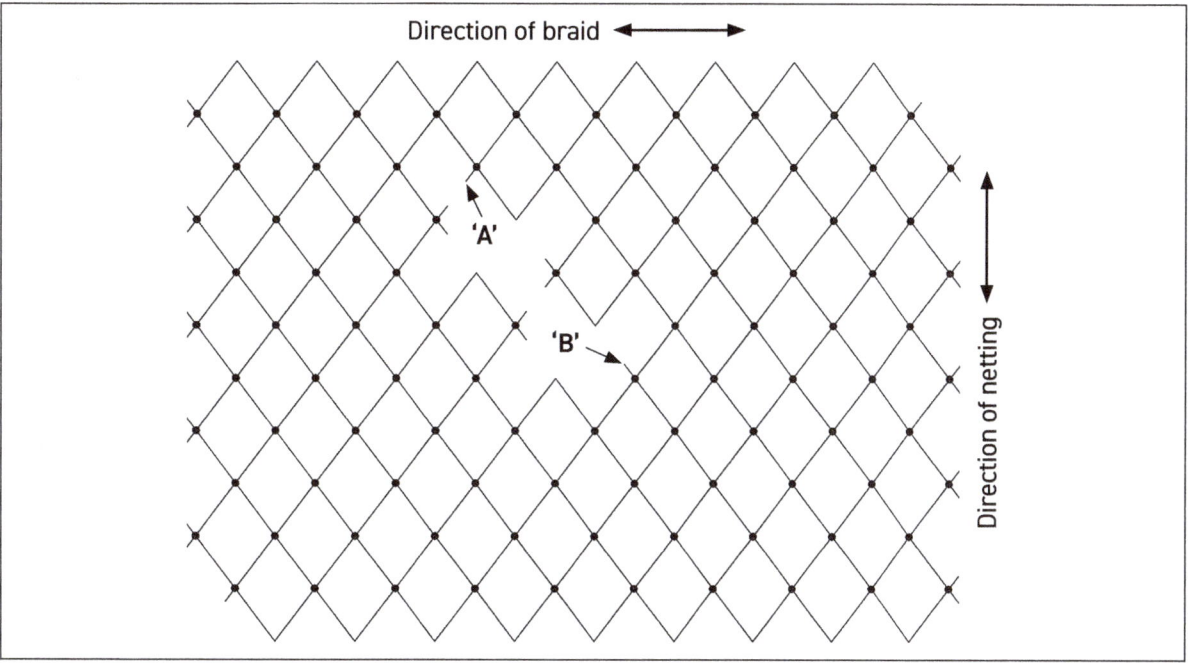

Figure 11.5

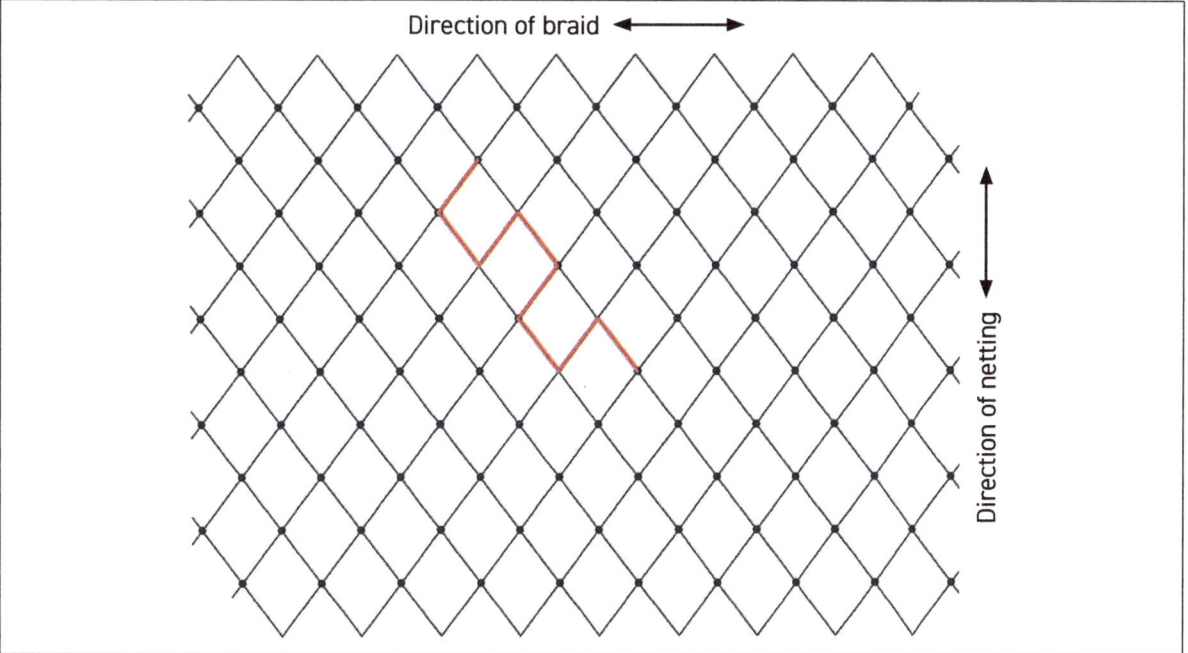

Figure 11.6

MAKING AND MENDING CAST NETS 59

Now let's get back to the tear shown in **Figure 11**.

In this case there is more than just a half mesh missing, there are whole meshes missing that will need to be braided back in, in order to repair the tear. In this case, a mesh stick is used to braid in the missing meshes. In using this technique, the repair is carried out in the direction of the netting, starting at **'A'** and finishing at **'B'**. **Figure 11.7** shows a net trimmed ready for repair, the same as that shown previously in **Figure 11**.

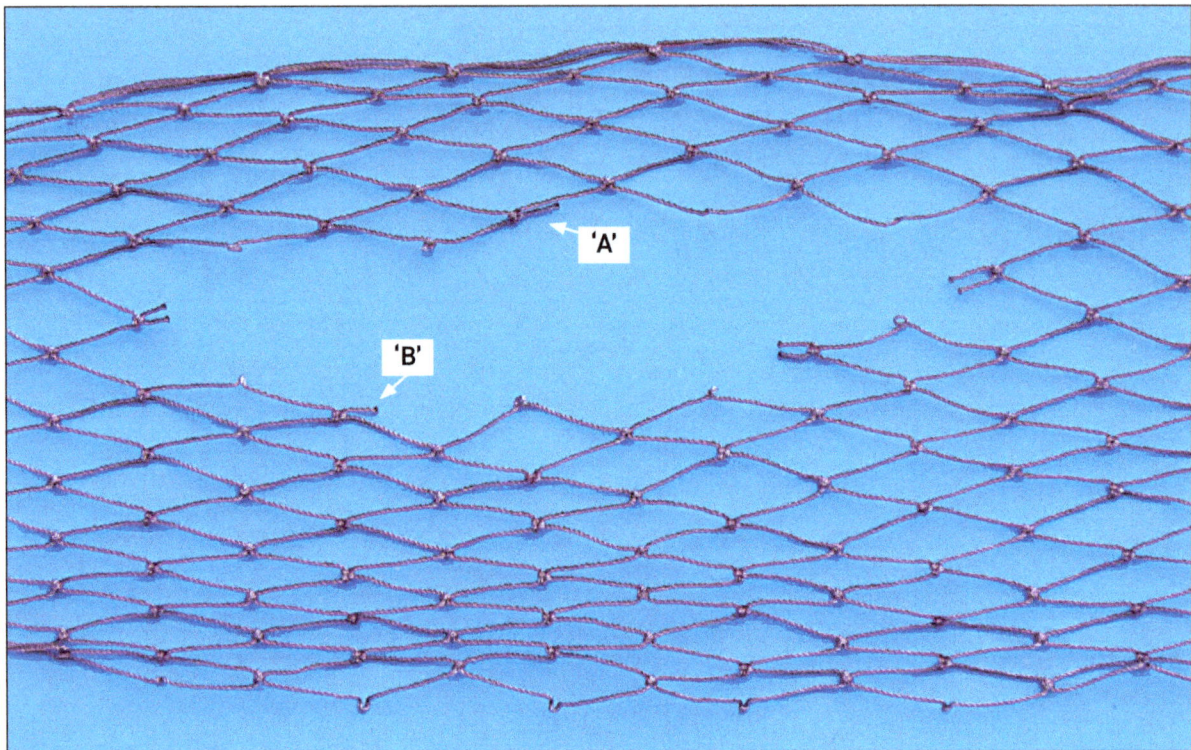

Figure 11.7

I will now take you through a step-by-step process to mend this tear.

1. Count up six meshes above the trimmed tear, and working in the direction of the braid, loop onto the wall hook sufficient meshes immediately above the trimmed tear. Repeat the same process below the trimmed tear for the waistline. **Figure 11.8** shows a section of netting set between the wall hook and waistline, or waistline hook in this case.

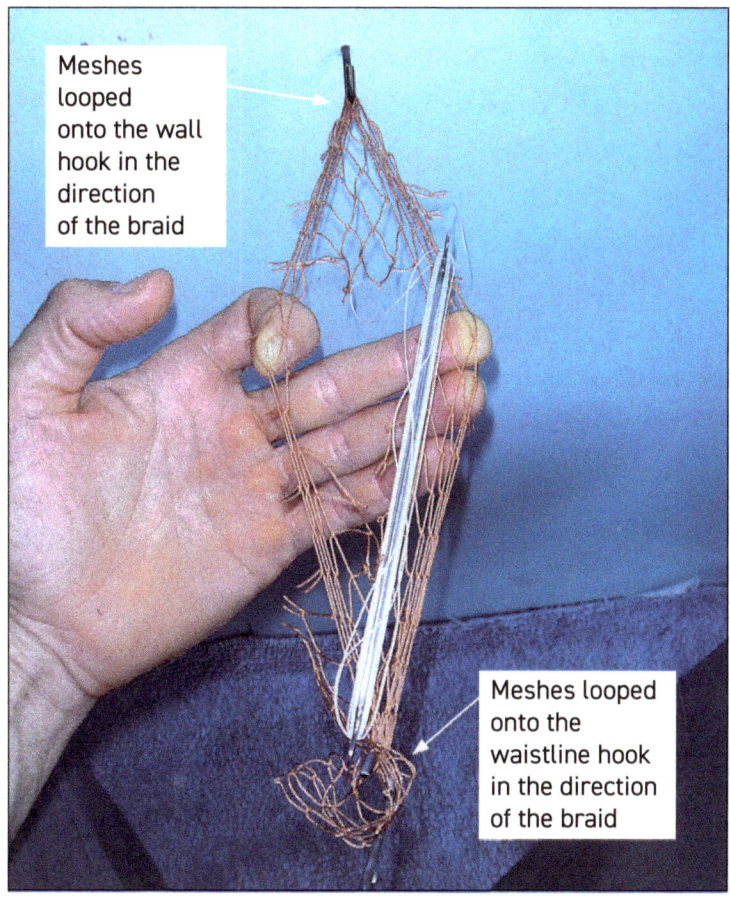

Figure 11.8

2. Tie off to the bar at point '**A**', using a starting knot, as shown in **Figure 11.9**.

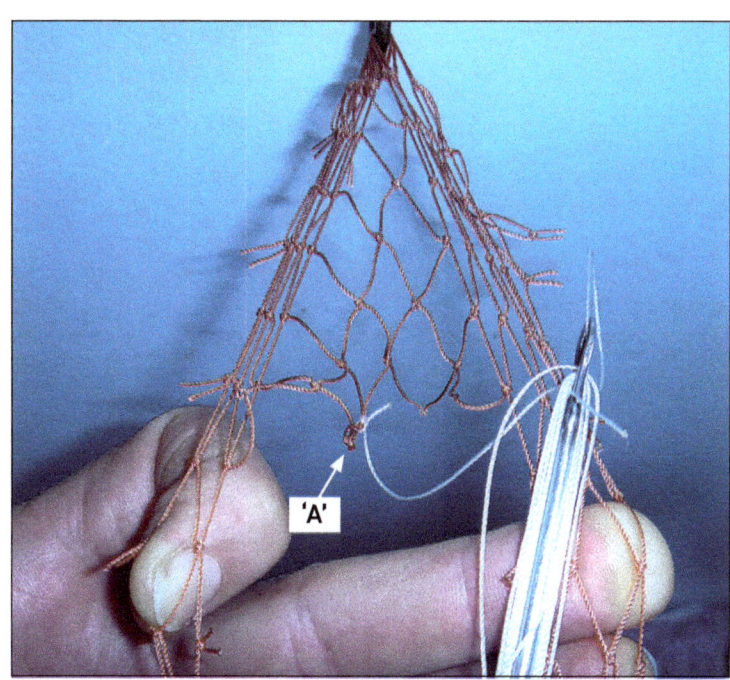

Figure 11.9

MAKING AND MENDING CAST NETS 61

3. Using a mesh stick with a cross section that has a perimeter equal to the size of the mesh being made, braid in a row of half meshes, working from left to right, as shown in **Figure 11.10**. **Figure 11.11** shows the finished half row of meshes. Here I have used a sheet bend knot to tie off to the cleaned meshes, but a flat knot would be just as good.

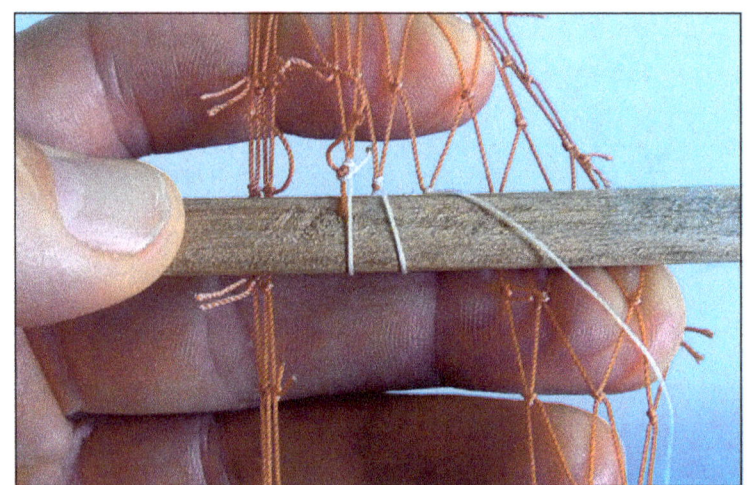

Figure 11.10

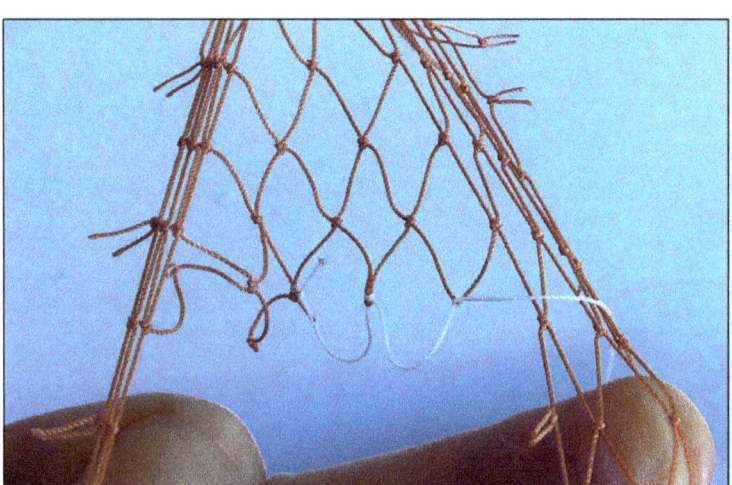

Figure 11.11

4. Tie off to the points mesh by using a side knot shown at point 'C', and then pick up the clean mesh, as shown at point 'D'. Now, again using the mesh stick and working from right to left, braid in the missing half row of meshes, as show in Figure 11.12.

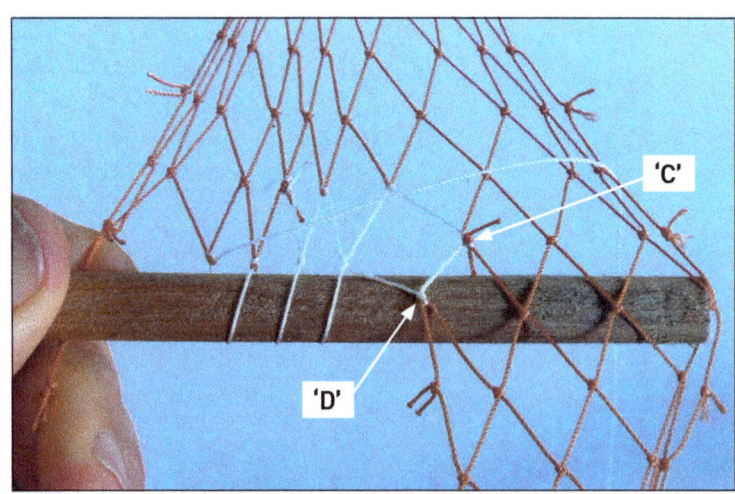

Figure 11.12

5. Repeat the operation as shown in Step 4, but this time you will be working from left to right. The end result is shown in **Figure 11.13** and **Figure 11.14**.

Figure 11.13

Figure 11.14

6. Once the missing meshes have been braided back in by using the mesh stick, as shown in **Figure 11.14**, all that remains is to braid in the missing half meshes, finishing at **'B'**, as shown in **Figure 11.15**.

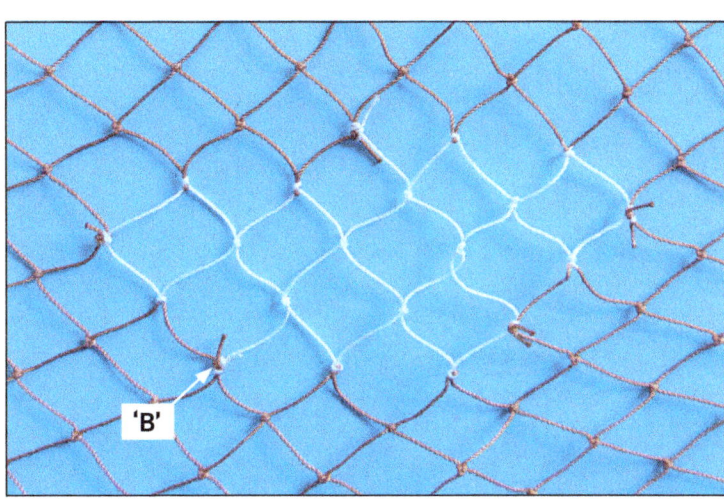

Figure 11.15

MAKING AND MENDING CAST NETS 63

REPAIRING LARGE TEARS

In the case of large tears, it is generally easer to insert a patch, than it is to braid in the missing meshes. The tear is trimmed to a rectangle or square shape without any bars, and the corresponding patch also has no bars, only whole meshes. The tear is trimmed to two all-points cuts and two all-cleaned mesh cuts, as shown in **Figure 11.16**. A patch is then cut from a separate piece of netting of the same mesh size. The patch is one whole mesh less than the trimmed tear and is cut to consist of two all-points cuts and two all-cleaned mesh cuts, as shown in **Figure 11.16** also.

To start this operation off, you will need to count up six meshes above the trimmed tear, and working in the direction of the braid, loop onto the wall hook sufficient meshes immediately above the trimmed tear, as previously shown in **Figure 11.8**. Then, as shown in Chapter 6, **Figure 6.14** and **Figure 6.15**, thread the waistline through the patch and tie the waistline off around your waist.

Now, using the wall hook and waistline to set the braid length, sew in the missing half mesh, starting at **'A'** and finishing at **'A'**. To carry out this operation you will need to shift the waistline a number of times to set the braid length, and sew in the missing half meshes. Chapter 6, **Figure 6.16** and **Figure 6.11** show similar operations. **Figure 11.17** shows the half mesh sewn in.

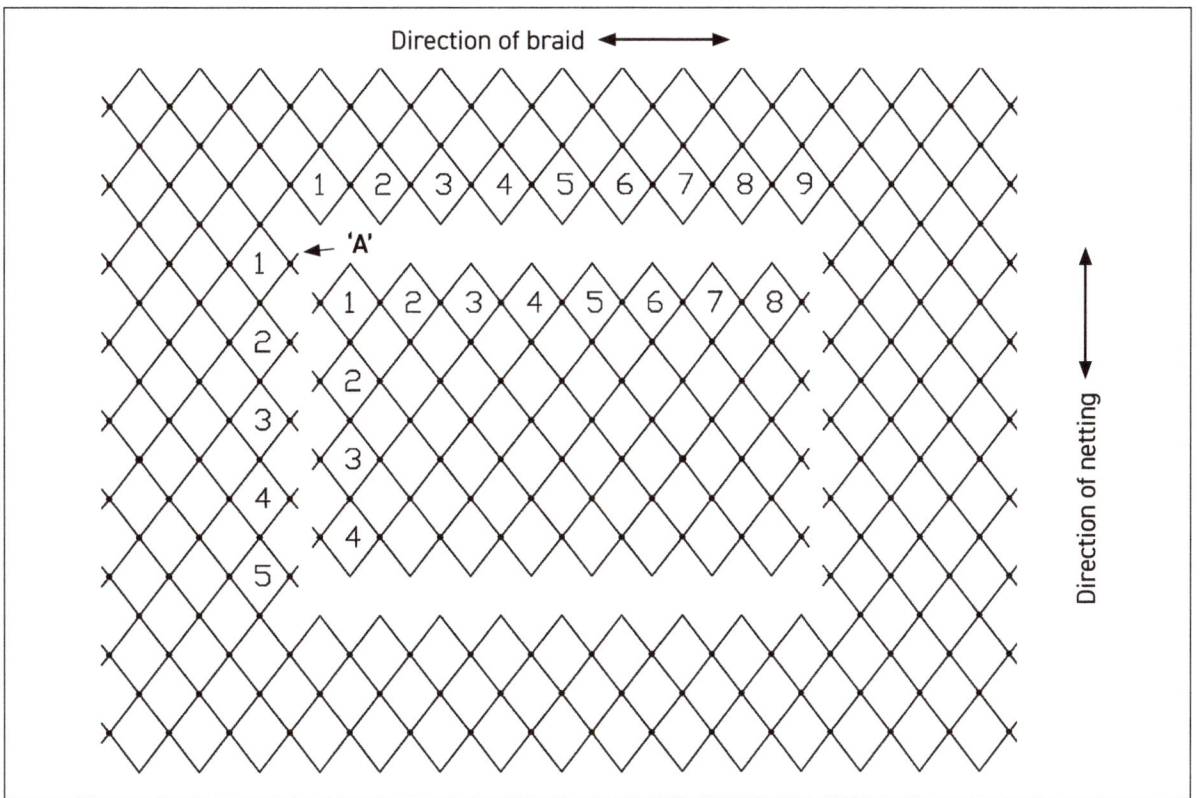

Figure 11.16

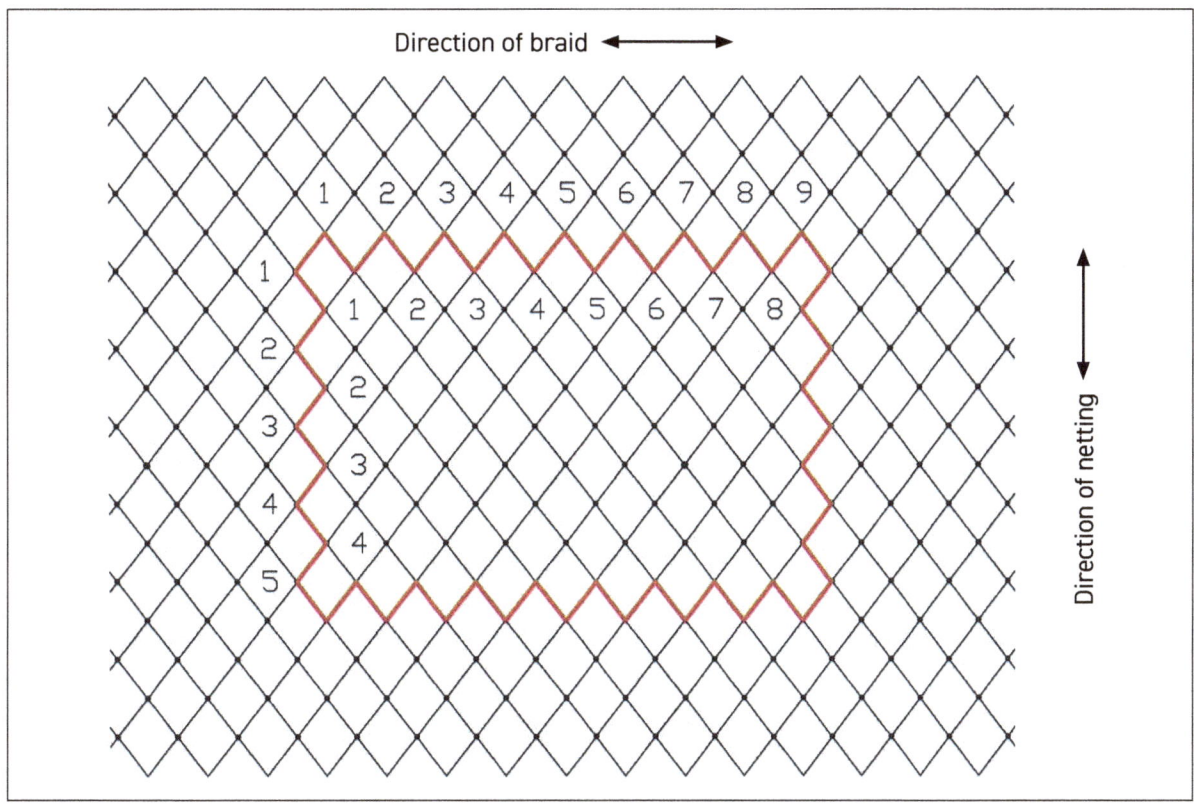

Figure 11.17

MAKING AND MENDING CAST NETS 65

TIPS FOR REPAIRING SMALL TEARS

Figure 11.18 shows a typical small horizontal tear. If you have not repaired your net on a regular basis, you can end up with a large number of these small tears. When using the wall hook and the waistline to set the braid length, I have found it very useful to have a hook on the waistline, as shown in **Figure 11.19**. This makes it easier and quicker to move from one tear to the next without having to untie and retie the waistline.

Figure 11.18

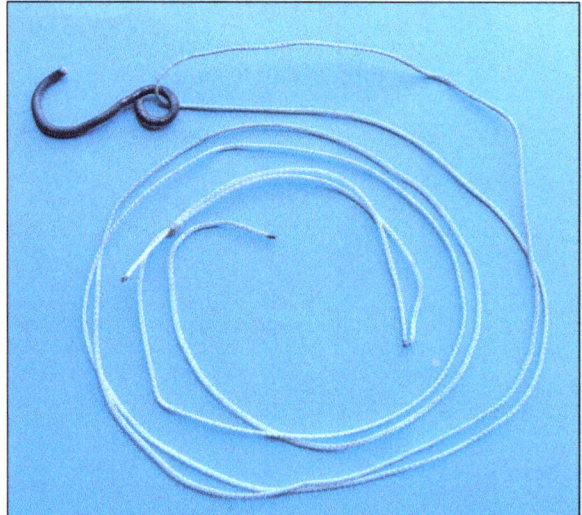

Figure 11.19

COMBINATION REPAIR

I must admit that I don't use this repair technique due to the stop–start nature of the repair, but I have shown it here for completeness of mending techniques.

As the name suggests, this repair is a combination of oblique, horizontal and vertical repair techniques, and it is completed in more than one step. **Figure 11.20** shows a combination tear that has been trimmed ready to braid in the missing half meshes.

Using a wall hook and waistline to set the braid length, braid in the missing half meshes by starting at '**A**' and finishing '**B**', and then start at '**C**' and finish at '**D**', and finally start at '**E**' and finish at '**F**'. **Figure 11.21** shows the half mesh sewn in.

In making the above statement, it is possible to continuously remake the net if you follow the leg of the mesh between '**B**' and '**D**', and '**C**' and '**E**', when starting at '**A**' and finishing at '**F**'. While the finish is a little untidy, it is an effective technique.

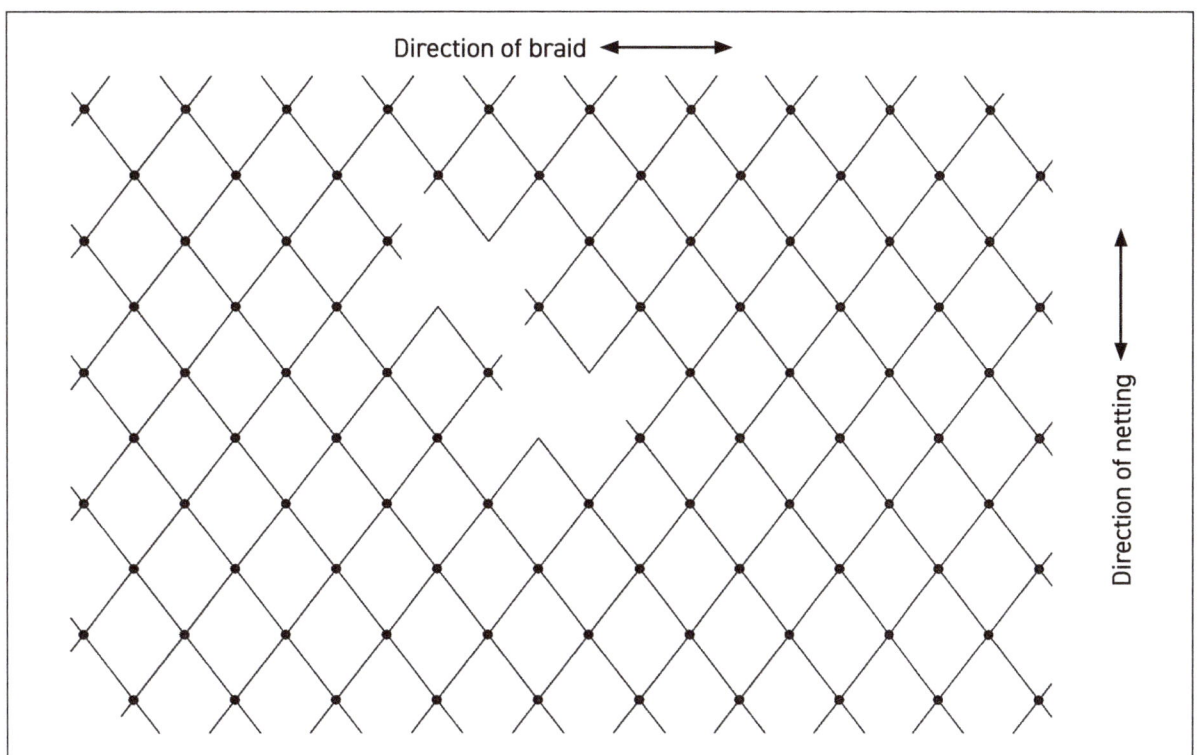

Figure 11.20

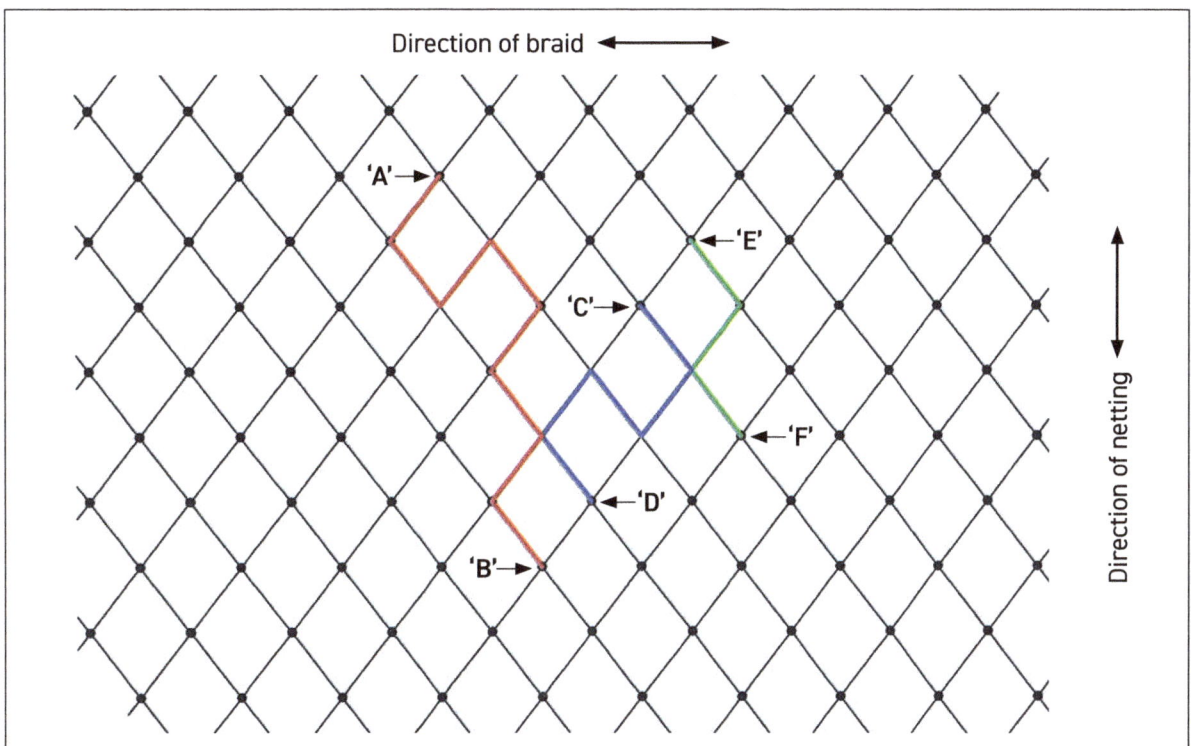

Figure 11.21

MAKING AND MENDING CAST NETS 67

12. MAKING A CAST NET TO SUIT YOUR INDIVIDUAL NEEDS

Some of you may remember the old ad on Australian TV: 'oils ain't oils'. Well the same applies here: 'nets ain't nets'.

You see, if you are casting a net up some little mangrove enclosed gutter 1.8 m (6 foot) wide, well there's no point in using a 6-m (20 foot) spread cast net, as you simply wouldn't have the room to spread it.

I have two cast nets that I use on a regular basis when I go fishing: one, 19-mm (¾ inch) mesh – 3-m (10 foot) spread cast net for chasing small baits and for using up small gutters where there is not much room to cast; and one, 25-mm (1 inch) mesh – 4.9-m (16 foot) spread cast net that I use not only as a general purpose net, but also for chasing larger fish out on the sand flats in more open water.

I will explain a little further by discussing mesh and net sizes (spreads) to suit different requirements.

A 19-mm (¾ inch) mesh cast net is ideal for chasing small baitfish and prawns (shrimp), if you are requiring small whole baits for the fish you are targeting.

A 25-mm (1 inch) mesh cast net is a good general-purpose mesh size that will allow the small baitfish and prawns to pass through, while still providing good baitfish for your days fishing.

This book does not cover mesh sizes beyond this point, but essentially as you go up in mesh size you are targeting bigger fish. Note, however, that regulations in your state, territory or country may limit the mesh size you are able to use. So you will need to contact your local authorities to find out what the regulations are in your area.

As to net size, or spread in this case, you have to consider not only where the net is intended to be cast, such as a small gutter or open water, but also the person who will be casting the net – whether or not they are a beginner, a child or adolescent, or someone with more experience that is used to handling a much larger net.

As a general guide, I would suggest the following:

1. A net up to 12-foot spread will be good for small gutters and more open water, and for a child or adolescent.

2. A net from 14-foot spread and up will be good for open water and anyone with a little more experience casting nets.

I would also like to touch on the pros and cons of multifilament and monofilament nylon material used to make cast nets. Functionally, the two materials do exactly the same job.

The advantage with multifilament nylon over monofilament nylon is that less net is required to make a cast net, but the disadvantage is that it holds water when in use, making it a little heavier when casting. It also has a tendency to be harder to remove baits, over the monofilament material. Therefore, when chasing prawns, monofilament is the preferred material.

13. HOW A NET WORKS

Many people are under the misconception that a cast net of 7-foot drop will give you a 14-foot spread. This is not true. You see, when a cast net is picked up at the head, the meshes are elongated, giving you the 7-foot drop.

But when a cast net is spread, the meshes of the cast net open up. And as they open up, the meshes shorten, thus shortening the overall spread of the cast net. The amount it shortens is dependent upon the net design, or more specifically, the amount of mesh allowed for in the design.

The difference can be quite significant. The cast net patterns in this book will give at least a true spread dimension to the inside diameter of the lead line, after allowing for the formed pocket and the reduction of the cast net when spread.

14. CARE AND MAINTENANCE

Generally speaking, the materials from which cast nets are made are practically imperious to rot, but there are still some good practices to adhere to.

1. Rinse the cast net out in fresh water, and remove any debris before hanging it out to dry.

2. Check the net for any tears and carry out the necessary repairs. It is better to carry out repairs after each use, as the job can become quite a major exercise if left.

3. Store the cast net out of direct sunlight and away from any chemicals that may deteriorate the material.

CONCLUSION

The ability to make and repair cast nets is unfortunately a dying trade in the more westernised civilisations. I have produced this book in an effort to try and capture this knowledge so that it may be passed onto interested generations to come.

I have deliberately not produced literature on the actual hand braiding of a cast net, as the availability of machine-made netting makes the task of making a cast net much easier.

REFERENCES

Department of Agriculture, Fisheries and Forestry, Queensland Government, viewed April 2015, <https://www.qld.gov.au/recreation/activities/boating-fishing/rec-fishing/rules/equipment>.

Libert. L, Maucorps. A & Innes. L 1987, *Mending of Fishing Nets*, 2nd edn, Fishing News Books Ltd, England.

Pawson, D 1998, *Handbook of Knots Expanded Edition*, Dorling Kindersley Limited, London.

ISO 3660:1976, *Fishing nets – Mounting and joining of netting – Terms and illustrations*, viewed November 2018, <https://www.iso.org/standard/9111.html>.

ISO 1531:1973, *Fishing nets – Hanging of netting – Basic terms and definitions*, viewed November 2018, <https://www.iso.org/standard/6120.html>.

My grandfather, Ron McFarlane (left), and myself (right).

www.ingramcontent.com/pod-product-compliance
Lightning Source LLC
Chambersburg PA
CBHW061537010526
44107CB00066B/2895